W9-ANQ-380

BURPEE AMERICAN GARDENING SERIES

VINES

BURPEE

AMERICAN GARDENING SERIES

VINES

Suzanne Frutig Bales

MACMILLAN • USA

This book is dedicated to my son, the family musician, Carter Franklin Bales II.

MACMILLAN • USA
A Prentice Hall Macmillan Company
15 Columbus Circle
New York, NY 10023

Copyright © 1995 by Suzanne Frutig Bales

All rights reserved, including the right to reproduce this book or portions thereof in any form whatsoever.

MACMILLAN is a registered trademark of Macmillan, Inc.

Library of Congress Cataloging-in-Publication Data

Bales, Suzanne Frutig.
    Vines / Suzanne Frutig Bales.
        p.   cm.—(Burpee American gardening series)
    Includes index.
    ISBN 0-02-860037-1
    1. Ornamental climbing plants. 2. Ornamental
climbing plants—
    Pictorial works. I. Title. II. Series.
    SB427.B28   1995
    635.9'74—dc20   94-5195
                                          CIP

Designed by Levavi & Levavi

Manufactured in the United States of America

10 9 8 7 6 5 4 3 2 1

Burpee is a registered trademark of W. Atlee Burpee and Company.

Cover photograph by Horticulture Photography, Corvallis, Oregon.

All other photographs by Suzanne Frutig Bales, except photo page 32 by Kay Reeves and photo page 66 by Allen Roach.

I would like to thank the many people who have helped me. My thanks go to my husband Carter; my gardening partner, Martha Kraska; and my assistant Gina Norgard for providing me with unending help and support. Many thanks also go to the garden designers and gardeners whose gardens appear in this book: Laurie and John Barry, Robert Dash, Bob Titus, Charles Cresson, Marco Polo Stuffano, Wave Hill, Bayberry Nursery, Meadow Brook farm, Lindon Pennock, Jack Lenor Larson, J. Barry Ferguson, The Brooklyn Botanic Garden, Carol Prisant, and Tish Rehill.

Again, as in my other books, I want to thank my father, Edward C. Frutig, who graciously gave freely of his time to help me shape the book.

Previous page: A variety of vines cover the author's trellis, providing a shady place to stroll or sit while enjoying a succession of bloom from spring to fall. The assortment of vines includes climbing roses, wisteria, honeysuckle and clematis.

CONTENTS

INTRODUCTION

Vines are more touched by wonder, beauty and even mystery than any other kind of plant I know. Vines are the garden's acrobats and gymnasts, easily executing high-wire feats. They turn and flip over with ease, in perfect cartwheels and back bends. They scamper across mats of grass, leap over streams, dangle from cliffs, shimmy up trees and somersault back down, twisting and turning gracefully as they go.

The only difficulty with vines is choosing among their many beautiful forms. There are the blaring trumpets of mandevilla, allamander and hummingbird vine, the flat, salad-plate-sized faces of large-flowered clematis and moonflower, the smaller smiling faces of black-eyed Susan vine and morning glory, the nodding bells of Oriental clematis, and the curls of confetti on Japanese honeysuckle. Common names offer apt descriptions for some of the more complex flower designs: cup-and-saucer vine, bleeding heart vine, climbing snapdragon, Dutchman's pipe, paper flower, balloon vine, canary-bird and fleece vine.

Of course, vines are more than just pretty faces. Many are grown for their foliage, whether it be evergreen or deciduous. Vines can be a background or stage set for a garden, rising above it to add height, color and beauty while softening and decorating hard surfaces. Vines grown for their foliage include delicate lacy akebia, shiny, leathery English ivy, creeping fig with its tiny green hearts, golden hops and even golden ivies. In fall, many of the deciduous vines change color before they undress for winter. Virginia creeper and Boston ivy wear fall's fiery colors and are among the most flamboyantly dressed.

The possibilities with vines seem limitless. The old saying, "the path to heaven is beneath you," makes me think of vines. Vines draw the eye toward heaven, grabbing a little of the sky and bringing it closer to earth, and a touch of heaven is what a garden is all about. With the combined effects of their height, color and often fragrance, vines create the illusion of greater size in the smallest garden. Vines seem to cause boundaries to expand while they give a garden definition. Even a small garden appears larger when vines direct the eye upward to flowers blooming overhead. They can tie the entire garden together with a background of tropical lushness, and they direct attention to the beauty of all the flowers. Adding brilliant or subtle color to your landscape, they give your garden a "finished" look. With a touch of extravagance, flowering vines decorate and beautify or, in the case of ivy, dapperly clothe what they cover.

The higher-growing vines with showy flowers—wisteria, trumpet vine, roses, bittersweet—provide impact even from a distance. The eye will keep going to them. Vines are living sculpture, focal points in the garden. A gazebo canopied with lush foliage becomes a green or flowering bower. An arbor covered with vines focuses the view and frames a vista. A glimpse through a vine-covered arch to an inviting pathway or garden brings enchantment and mystery. A series of arbors or arches, planted with fragrant vines, becomes a perfumed passage. What could bring more pleasure than sitting or strolling beneath a canopy of flowers? Frequently vines are used to conceal or camouflage the unsightly. My family discovered an old stone gardener's shed left by previous owners on our property with ivy growing up over the roof, hiding its holes. Though the shed was no longer functional, it was picturesque.

Finally, there's the mystery of vines. No one knows why hops insist on twining clockwise as they climb, while morning glories twine counterclockwise. If gently unwound and twined in the opposite direction, both vines slowly unwrap, then rewrap in their preferred direction.

With so much to offer and so many varieties, why is it vines seem all but forgotten, the last planted and the least thought about? Garden on the fence, up a wall, over an existing shrub or tree. Allow a vine to sprawl over a rocky area or cover a steep bank. As you add a vine or two, or three, you'll find your garden never had it so lush nor looked so beautiful. Although it is often cautioned that "for the most pleasing effect in a garden, use restraint," I'll never accept it. When it comes to vines, more is better.

In their trumpet vine–covered gazebo, Laurie and John Barry enjoy meals as well as reflective moments.

PLANNING AND DESIGNING WITH VINES

VINES DEFINED

A vine, as defined by Webster, is a climbing plant that bears grapes. Gardeners often use "vines" as a catch-all word to describe plants too wobbly to stand alone. For their vertical growth vines need another plant or a structure to climb on, or a gardener to lend them a helping hand. In short, vines are climbers. "Vine" is not a precise term, nor is it a scientific category. Many a vine, bougainvillea, for example, can be pruned to be a fullsome shrub or allowed to sprawl as a groundcover. Conversely, a shrub such as *Pyracantha coccinea* planted against a wall may climb up to 20 feet, yet it is not listed as a vine. Whether a plant grows as a vine or not is determined sometimes by cultural practices, sometimes by its environment. Vines climb for the promise of light. They have adapted to the competition of other plants by sending their roots deeper into the ground to seek water and nutrition, while holding their heads higher to bask in the sun. In the humid tropics, innumerable types of vines developed through the need to compete with an overpopulation of plants for sunlight, food and water. The farther we move from the equator, the fewer vines we find.

Still, decorative vines grow everywhere. Some vines are cherished for their flowers, others for their fruit, foliage, or perhaps their autumn coloring. No matter where you live, the choices are staggering as you select from short and chubby or tall and slim vines, annual or perennial vines, woody or herbaceous vines, evergreen or deciduous vines, and vines with flowers that bloom in virtually any color. The foliage may be any shade of green, through golds and burgundies, and variegated, too. As they move, whether by limping or leaping, many naturally twist, twine and tangle, adding graceful lines and a softening touch to the garden.

Vines can grow up fences and walls, hang down from window boxes and hanging baskets, circle around poles and buildings or lie spread-eagled on the ground. Plant vines to decorate fences and walls, to mask unsightly outbuildings, on arbors and pergolas for shade and beauty, and to sprawl as groundcovers and hold banks or weave plants together. Some plants need almost as much underground space for their feet as for their heads. Not vines. Vines are nature's over-achievers, adding lushness to the garden while taking relatively little room for their feet. They grow to great size from roots a fraction of the size of their bodies. A climbing

A mixture of annual and perennial vines lushly cover the author's lattice gazebo. The pink roses, gold-net honeysuckle and white clematis return each year, complemented this year by annual red and blue sweet peas.

annual vine may grow 20 feet or more in one summer, a perennial vine higher yet, each using only a square foot or two of ground.

Most vines prefer their feet in the shade and their heads in the sun. This characteristic makes them easy to combine with other plants, particularly at the back of a garden. Many vines develop bare legs if grown behind other plants; as they climb, they seem to broaden at the "hips"; this characteristic can be used to advantage when a vine is grown behind a wide shrub to climb up a wall. Some vines are willing to climb through the shade of tall trees, growing 40 feet or more before reaching much-needed sun. Once they reach the sun, they put on a dazzling display of flowers.

LEANERS, TWINERS, GRASPERS AND CLINGERS

Vines vary greatly in the way they climb. Large-flowered clematis and love-in-a-puff tread lightly, calmly threading their way over, around and through their hosts, the plants that literally support them. Stiff-legged climbing roses lean against a wall. Ivy clings as it slowly creeps up any available surface. Morning glories twine around their support, which is why they are so popular on mailbox posts. A few vines behave badly, kudzu and honeysuckle being the most notorious. They stomp through the South suffocating, choking and mangling all in their path. Kudzu, an agricultural miracle in Japan, turned into a monster in the southern United States, where it has been named "the vine that ate the South." More about this in the chapter Vine Portraits. Take the time to understand how a vine climbs before you plant it. In the wrong place, a vine can turn into a gluttonous monster, or it may fail to perform and lie limp.

Lest I scare you, let me say that vines are among the easiest and showiest of plants to grow. Vines are adaptable; they have to be, as over time they had to find ways to reach sunlight. The methods vines use to climb can be loosely categorized as the leaners, the twiners, the graspers, and the clingers. The leaners include the climbing roses, although some such as *Rosa* 'American Pillar' are able to pull themselves up by snagging their hooks on another plant or trellis. As leaners grow, they need to be fastened to a support. The twiners climb by twining their stems up and around. These include the honeysuckles, morning glories and wisteria. They climb as high as there is a support for them to twine about, then proceed to twine back down around themselves. The graspers are similar to the twiners, climbing by means of tendrils that grab and twist around supports. The tendrils have been compared to coiled springs, pigs' tails and corkscrews. Both clematis and grapes grab and twist around their supports. The clingers anchor themselves by means of little holdfasts that look like suction cups. Included in this group are ivies, Virginia creeper and climbing hydrangea. Clingers climb surfaces from masonry to tree trunks, but are best grown on brick or stone walls. They should be watched, and in many cases controlled, to keep them below the roof line. They have the dangerous ability to "raise the roof" as they pull off shingles or even boards on a clapboard house.

Climbing hydrangea (Hydrangea anomala petiolaris) sends out aerial rootlets or fastholds along its stem to cling to any surface it climbs. Here it is climbing a stucco wall.

DESIGNING WITH VINES

Many gardeners like to keep their garden's gaiety a surprise, visible only after a visitor actually enters the garden, often hidden at the rear of the property. I say, plant elaborately in front of the house, and share the beauty of your garden with all who pass by. Give everyone something to smile about! Perhaps this way the gardening spirit will be passed along and cause a flurry of activity to beautify front yards with pretty gardens, rather than just the

Button supports (available at nurseries) can be glued to most surfaces to hold upright those vines that lean, such as the climbing rose pictured here.

usual shrubs and grass.

If a house is picturesque, a climbing rose or clematis (or both) trained over a doorway or porch will lend it charm; if not, a green climber such as Boston or English ivy will make it seem to recede into its surroundings while window boxes overflowing with colorful flowers lend their charm. Of course, once the ivy is established, a flowering vine on top would be quite an unusual and dramatic accent. A layering of vines is a practical beautification, one that requires some patience and time to become established (see "A Happy Tangle of Vines," page 15). Fences surrounding small yards are more attractive with shorter vines entwined about their posts. Easy annual vines, love-in-a-puff, scarlet runner beans and morning glories, and perennial vines such as large-flowered clematis and one of the shorter hybrid honeysuckles are ideal for this.

Look around your home, front and back, and you'll see many places for growing vines. Consider lamp posts, fences, the walls or posts of a building, existing shrubs, trees, and even other vines, such as climbing roses, that will easily support a limp-limbed vine. A birdhouse on a tall pole can be attractively placed at one end of a border or in the middle of a circular garden; the pole is then beautified by planting a twining vine at its feet. Ivy planted at the base of a garden sculpture will lightly drape or dress it without

Right: *Morning glories are one of the "twiners" that wrap their stems around supports. They grow as high as there is a support for them to climb, then proceed to twine back down around themselves. This birdhouse is located in one of the many beautiful gardens at Bayberry Nursery on Long Island.*

The fence around Bayberry Nursery's vegetable garden is decorated with morning glories too.

Clematis '*Jackmanii*' climbs a lamp post.

Pillars, with chains or ropes loosely draped between them, are favorites in older, formal gardens; most are planted with climbing roses that grow along them, but many other vines work just as well. At Old Westbury Gardens on Long Island, such chains hang at waist height at the back of the garden, where they provide a finishing edge that stops the eye from wandering onto the lawn beyond. The Cranford Memorial Rose Garden at the Brooklyn Botanic Garden uses similar supports, but here the pillars and chains are higher and the roses are strung overhead. There are many other uses for chains as well. Rain chains, especially weathered copper ones hanging from a gutter, offer a decorative place for vines to climb. The shorter climbers, which include most annuals, large-flowered clematis and many roses, form fanciful "curtains" for garden rooms. A climbing rose covers quite a large area when fanned out to be as wide as it is tall. Bloom proliferates on horizontally trained canes, where the plants receive more sun. Untrained, they reach straight for heaven and bloom only toward the top.

Climbers needn't be planted solely at the back of a garden. They can be trained to cover arbors, and if fragrant, will surround the casual stroller with delightful perfume. A garden seat with a canopy of vines trained overhead becomes a restful, fragrant and shady spot that welcomes the weary. Windows crowned with wreaths of roses decorate the outside of a

obscuring it. One gardener I know has a wooden horse's head mounted on a stable wall, and Dutchman's pipe is allowed to bridle it gently with a wreath. Poles arranged in the shape of a tepee may take on sculptural appeal when decorated with vines and placed in the center of a garden. At Wave Hill, a 28-acre public estate garden overlooking the Hudson River in New York City, tepees covered with clematis are prominent features in the flower garden.

In Carol Prisant's garden, a small-leaf ivy, planted at the base of a garden sculpture, dresses the sculpture without obscuring it.

At Wave Hill in New York City, clematis grown up a tepee structure fashioned of tree branches is the focal point of a mixed border.

house, floating fragrance indoors when the windows are open. To wake with a morning glory at your window is to start the day in a happy frame of mind. A garden gate canopied with a trellis of blooms is an invitation to enter. A tall fence decorated as an embroidered floral screen of flowering vines handsomely divides two outdoor areas. Ugly, bare walls disappear when festooned with garlands of flowering vines. These are the pleasures of vines.

Alice R. Ireys, a noted landscape architect, recommends growing a vine (frequently her choice is wisteria) as an "eyebrow" over a garage, to draw the eye up and away from the large, not particularly attractive door; the vine—especially when in bloom—is what is noticed and remembered. Once Ireys planted quick-growing fleece vine to cover an inexpensive railing that wound down a steep, shady hill, following a waterfall. The vine covering the railing blended with the natural setting, so that the stairs fit right into the hillside. When I saw it myself, I thought how pleasant it was to grab the cool, soft leaves.

Versatile vines can make excellent groundcovers, ivy being the one most commonly used this way. Ivy can provide a carpet where no grass will grow, rooting as it runs along the earth. Stairs, laced with ivy that is pruned to cover the risers, but not the stair treads, look carpeted in a formal fashion more popular with Victorians than the gardeners of

Vines add lushness to the garden. Here, Boston ivy covers a water tower, climbing roses bloom on trellises and annual vines are beginning to climb the series of arches in the cutting garden.

today. (For this effect, clip the ivy whenever it strays beyond a 10-inch limit.) Many of the flowering vines, such as the large-flowering clematis, are a pleasant surprise when allowed to weave along the ground, occasionally climbing up and over another flower. Small-flowered clematis can scramble down a bank or through a bed of ivy to add a little color to a shady area. Many rambler roses will successfully scramble over an embankment, preventing erosion as they grow and blooming with little or no care.

A trellis of climbing roses provides dappled shade and protection from the heat and burning rays of the sun. In the shade of the trellis daylilies bloom.

NATURE'S WAY

Even when not in bloom, fleece vine grown as an "eyebrow" over garage doors draws the eye up and away from the doors as it enhances the building.

In nature's way of combining plants, shrubs, trees and woody-stemmed vines are often living supports for loose-limbed, delicate vines; larger trees support woody vines. If the gardener follows nature's lead, vines create a sense of spontaneity in the garden. It is easier on the gardener if no separate structure is necessary. A vine planted on the north side of a shrub or tree will have its roots shaded and cool, a desirable situation. Depending on the color of its foliage, the host plant may provide a restful, dense green backdrop perfect for displaying any flower, or a bold contrast, as with the purple foliage of smoke bush (*Cotinus coggygria* 'Purpureus') or the golden foliage of *Spiraea × bumalda* 'Gold Flame'.

Many annual vines clothe and costume as they thread their way around and up host plants. They never cause trouble. They can easily grow up small

Clematis 'Marie Boisselot' blooms in late spring, climbing a shrub and trailing onto the ground as a flowering groundcover. Alliums bloom at the front.

trees, through and over shrubs, and up climbing roses. Clematis, like other flowering vines, can make a spring-flowering shrub appear to be in bloom at an off time of year. Forsythia, for example, which blooms in early spring, could be covered with the large purple flowers of *Clematis* × 'Jackmanii' from June to September. Balloon vine is a bit player rather than a scene stealer, gentle in its caresses, delicate with ferny foliage and starry white flowers. I have yet to see it where it doesn't add interest. Moonflower and morning glory are more aggressive. They are good choices for large northern shrubs but can be trouble in the South, where they grow with abandon.

A tree festooned with blossoms is a beautiful sight. For this lovely effect, don't neglect (as I did) to consider the bloom times of the tree and vine. I once planted *Clematis montana* on an ornamental cherry; the

tree and the clematis both bloom with small pink flowers, usually at the same time of year, making it hard to tell them apart. What with this lack of planning, the vine goes unnoticed most years. When—occasionally—-the clematis stays in bloom longer, I am reminded of what could have been, had I planted sweet autumn clematis to light the tree with small, sweetly scented flowers at summer's end, or *Clematis orientalis* for its summery yellow bells. For maximum beauty, plan for the vine to bloom at a different time than the tree, which gives the impression that the tree is in bloom again. You can plan for all-summer bloom if annual vines are planted on a spring-blooming shrub or non-flowering tree. Or, you might plan for simultaneous bloom, but be smarter than I was; select a vine with a contrasting color and shape of flower.

Here on Long Island, it used

Many vines thread their way around and up other plants, enhancing the beauty of each. Pictured here, the purple double clematis 'Vyvyan Pennell' grows up and through the shrub rose 'Bonica'.

to be fashionable to plant a wisteria to grow up a locust tree. The wisteria would bloom first, and then when its flowers faded, the locust leaves opened. As the foliage of the locust and the wisteria are similar, it was difficult to tell the two apart, and it looked as though the tree were blooming early. The result was an extended season of bloom. Trumpet vine is another woody-stemmed vine that can climb a tall tree for summer bloom. If the tree has dense branches and branches close to the ground, careful pruning might be necessary to allow more light and a clearer path for the vine.

When planting a vine to climb a tree, many garden writers advise starting at the drip line of the tree's branches, and training the vine up a stick or cord to the lowest branches. I feel the look of a vine growing at the outskirts of a tree and then up into its branches is not as attractive as if a vine is

grown to hug the trunk as it climbs. For a natural and more attractive look, I prefer it when a vine climbs a tree's trunk. Planting close to the trunk, among the larger tree roots, is not a problem if you have sufficient room to dig and prepare the soil. Here, the tree roots are not sapping nutrients and water from the soil in this area. Planting at the drip line of the branches places the vine among the tree's feeder roots. Another way to plant a vine to climb a tree, if too many roots are close to the trunk, is to plant where it is easy to dig and prepare the soil, then lay the stem of the vine underground for a few feet so that it emerges close to the tree trunk. A cane or a wire can guide the vine from the ground to the tree. This method works especially well with clematis, and in fact it prevents clematis wilt from killing the vine, because the underground portion of the stem will send up new shoots.

Climbing hydrangea (Hydrangea anomala petiolaris) *can climb any surface, including the trunks of trees.*

A HAPPY TANGLE OF VINES

With obvious differences in style, temperament and climbing techniques, various vines will beautifully and romantically twist and climb one another in combinations as lavish as embroidery. Most vines do not resent a close neighbor, and there are many clever combinations to try. I inherited a red climbing rose, the name of which I never discovered. Its feet are firmly planted at the back of a mixed flower border, taking up practically no space at all. The rose blooms once in

June, high up above a window on a wall covered with ivy. The dark red blooms practically jump off the wall in contrast to the dark green, shiny background of the dense-growing Boston ivy. As the flower petals fall, the climbing rose recedes into the background, and if it has any diseases (blackspot or mildew are common), I don't know about them, thanks to the ivy camouflage. The ivy and rose have a happy marriage; their lives have been compatibly intertwined for more than

Scarlet runner bean and morning glories, both annual vines, twist and tangle together to lavishly embroider a rustic fence by summer's end.

Gold-net honeysuckle's yellow-veined leaves brighten the flowers of the sweet pea vine they twine around.

By summer's end the arches in the author's cutting flower garden are covered with hyacinth bean, sweet peas and scarlet runner bean.

40 years. Another loving pair is the morning glory and moonflower. They too are like an old married couple, compatible because one works nights and the other works days. The morning glory opens with the first bright sunshine and, if the day isn't too hot or sunny, closes at twilight. The moonflower opens as the afternoon wanes and, for a few glorious hours, the two party together. Then the moonflower takes center stage to shine in the moonlight.

A clematis of mine that languished for several years on a trellis at the back of a border was lent a helping hand by a climbing rose. Growing up one side of the garden wall, the rose reached over the wall and down the other side to lift the clematis' flowers to new heights. Climbing roses can serve a dual purpose when used as trellises for other vines. Once a climbing rose is well established, its strong canes easily support weaker climbers. A large-flowered clematis (the small-flowered kinds usually grow too densely), morning glory, love-in-a-puff or other flexible-stemmed vine will add blossoms later in the summer to a climbing rose. A favorite combination of mine is *Rosa* 'Golden Showers' with the rich, lavender-blue *Clematis* 'Ramona' to clothe her bare legs. Charles Cresson, a noted garden writer, recommends growing *Lonicera sempervirens* over the carmine-pink Rosa 'Zephirine Drouhin'. He says, "The two make a striking display in late May; the coral honeysuckle is predominantly orange, but the base of each flower is the same pink as the rose, a color combination I would generally find difficult, but is delightful here. The contrasting flower forms add further charm."

Before combining vines, there are some practical considerations to note. Knowing the characteristics, probable height and color of each is important for planning. Sometimes their differences actually make them compatible. Variegated ampelopsis, for example, produces foliage on new growth. Left to its own devices, it will grow tall with umbrella foliage across the top. This effect could be an advantage in the right spot, perhaps a crowded area with no room for foliage near the ground; it would allow a shorter vine, such as clematis, morning glory, love-in-a puff or hyacinth bean, to climb its limbs. To encourage foliage from the bottom of the vine on up, it must be pruned almost to the ground each year. When pruned yearly, it grows up faster than most annual vines and will still intermingle. The height and the density of the "guest" vine is important. Don't invite a burdensome guest that stays too long, eats too much and weighs heavily on the host. A vine such as kudzu or Hall's honeysuckle would choke any host, growing too densely and blocking out the host vine's sunlight. A simple rule to follow when combining vines you don't know well is to choose only one that has stiff, woody stems; otherwise, you might have a battle of quiet intensity and strong wills, as the two woody vines try to strangle each other. There are some woody vine combinations that work if the trunks of the vines are kept separated (planted a minimum of 3 to 4 feet apart, depending on the vines), and only the arms allowed to wrap around each other. Fleece vine and trumpet vine together, for example, can be a stunning sight that contrasts frothy white flowers with solid orange or red trumpets.

Woody stems leave the gardener no choice but to chop them down if they become too unruly. Soft-stemmed, loose-limbed vines have the flexibility to be prodded gently in another direction at any time in their growth cycle. Loose, flexible-stemmed vines can be jumbled together, planted closer than commonly recommended, for a luxuriant look. If the tangle becomes more than the gardener wants, individual stems are easily snipped off or, if one is patient, unwound and spread out. Climbing roses have strong, woody stems and a stiff (but good) posture when properly supported. They have the strength to be good hosts for some of the shorter, better-behaved honeysuckles, large-flowered clematis and many short and sweet annual vines.

The choice of vine combinations varies greatly with climate and location. There are wonderful opportunities everywhere. The yellow jasmine, *Gelsemium sempevirens*, deserves recognition, blooming beautifully as early as February in Florida and April on Long Island. Not much else blooms that early to tangle with it on Long Island, but in Florida the rich yellow trumpet flowers contrast glowingly when combined with lavender-blue plumbago. But then, the blue of plumbago goes with everything from climbing roses of any color to morning glories and jasmine. Vines of similar growth habits can be grown together along a fence, over a trellis, up a post, as a wall tapestry (remember, plant closer than instructed to on the seed pack or per your planting guide for this special effect).

GUIDE FOR VINE COMBINATIONS

1. Many perennial vines, climbing roses and trumpet vine included, develop bare, woody bottoms as they grow older. These are natural trellises for shorter, softer-stemmed vines such as large-flowered clematis, love-in-a-puff and morning glories.

2. Height is a guide to combining vines. Any of the annual vines growing approximately the same height can be planted together for a rich tapestry of foliage and flowers. I prefer them planted closer together, usually a foot or two apart, rather than the 3 feet many planting instructions recommend; their roots don't need more space than this, and I like the twining effect as they climb.

3. Plan the colors of the vines to be combined as carefully as you plan the colors of your wardrobe. Do you want discreet color, a combination of fragile pastel as in a faded floral fabric, or do you want opulent, bold and brazen colors, perhaps the orange and purple of royalty, or the intense crayon colors loved by the young? Lively clashes of color can be exhausting or exhilarating, so plan carefully.

4. The amount of sun or shade vines will receive in a proposed planting spot should be determined, and the requirements of

Above: *Clematis are gentle vines when grown as nature intended, using other plants as trellises. Here,* Clematis *'Hagley Hybrid' blooms through* Rosa *'White Meidiland'.*

Above: *The scarlet morning glory grows up and over the perennial sweet autumn clematis.*

Above: *Sweet autumn clematis and 'Heavenly Blue' morning glory cover a fence together at summer's end.*

Left: *The seedpods of* Clematis orientalis *are almost as decorative as its nodding yellow flowers. The yellow climbing rose is tied to the wall, and the clematis uses it as a trellis to twine around.*

vines should be coordinated with the site.

5. The time of day the vine blooms and the season of bloom are important in coordinating one vine with its partner.

6. How each vine climbs may determine its success in a particular spot. A climbing hydrangea with aerial rootlets that cling to any surface, for example, wouldn't be a good choice if you want a vine to grow down the sides of a container, or to grow over another vine or up a trellis. All a climbing hydrangea needs is a bare wall. However, climbing hdyrangea that is well established on a wall can act as a trellis for another vine that climbs by grasping.

7. Is the structure supporting the vines something that will need to be repainted or repaired? If so, choose annual vines or perennial vines that can be removed easily and set on the ground, or cut to the ground. Ivy, fleece vine and sweet autumn clematis are some vines that will not be killed but will grow up from the roots again when cut to the ground.

8. Consider how fast the vine you want grows, and how tall it will ultimately be, when deciding what structure it is to grow on. A 6-foot-tall vine is perfect on a picket fence, but looks a little lost on the side of a house. Conversely, a vine that grows 20 feet tall is ideal on a house or grown along a long picket fence. If a cement-block building is an eyesore, you might not want to wait several years to see it covered. For this, choose a quick-growing vine such as fleece vine or hops, rather than climbing hydrangea or creeping fig.

A SCENTED GARDEN

A garden is at its best if it is a feast for the eyes and the nose. Fragrance is long remembered, sometimes even after images of the garden are forgotten. Today's roses and honeysuckles are not all fragrant, as is commonly thought. In fact, many are scentless. In the case of many modern roses, scent has been sacrificed for preferred colors and larger flowers. Fragrance is a recessive trait, and thus two deeply fragrant parents often produce a scentless offspring. Pink and red roses are the most highly scented, while white and yellow roses are rarely fragrant. Since the scent of most flowers is in the petals rather than the foliage, it follows that the double flowers, having more petals, are more fragrant, although the intensity and quality of the scent varies with the flower.

The intensity of the perfume of fragrant vines ranges from the obvious to the subtle. The fragrances of Hall's honeysuckle, sweet autumn clematis, wisteria, sweet pea, jasmine, *Stephanotis* and moonflower are loud, obvious and heady. From their perches, these vines breathe their sweet breath toward garden visitors; often as not, you can detect the fragrance before you see the vine. Shyer, more discreet vines, akebia and the cup-and-saucer among them, hide their fragrance from all but those close by; sometimes it's necessary to bury your nose in their bloom to enjoy their perfume. Both honeysuckle and jasmine smell strongest in the cool of night, and moonflower is fragrant only at night. Wisteria, on the other hand, has a stronger fragrance during the day. While there is no real pattern to the fragrance of the rose family, the diversity is intriguing. Some roses are fragrant in the morning, others are more fragrant a few days after opening, and many lose their fragrance as the individual flowers age.

The only way to differentiate one fragrance from another is to compare them to more familiar ones, and I find I usually associate floral fragrances with food. To me akebia has a simply sweet smell, sweet autumn clematis a vanilla scent, and *Clematis montana* 'Wilsonii' a chocolate scent. What is appealing to one person may not be to another. Many jasmines are recognized by their sweet floral scents, but the odd odor of Dutchman's pipe puts some people off.

Fragrance is fickle, varying with the weather. It is most pronounced and travels farthest on days that are warm and moist. Some warm and misty summer mornings I wake to the fragrance of honeysuckle wafting in my upstairs window. This is one of the few vines that, when planted at the back of a house, can often be smelled at the front of the house. The heat and drought of summer can repress the scent of the flowers. Wander through a flower garden on an oppressively hot day, and you'll find their fragrance is barely perceptible. The same is true on cold, cloudy days—the fragrance of all flowers decreases. Fragrance flourishes following a summer shower and after a light frost. The fragrance of a vine growing in the middle of a "wind tunnel" will ride off with the wind. In a protected corner, a vine curling around a garden seat shares its perfume with a guest. An arbor of fragrant roses, wisteria or jasmine offers a perfumed passage. Inside a gazebo the air may be perfumed most delightfully. And as I've said, when you plant fragrant vines under windows that are open in summer, you'll enjoy their perfume both inside the house and out.

The foregoing is only a sampling of fragrant vines to tweak your nose. For a time, at least, smell every flower you see. A nose needs exercise! It would be sad to think that, for lack of use, you might miss the pleasure of fragrance in the garden. The next time you see a flowering vine, stand back and breathe deeply, or better yet, run up and bury your nose in it. The pleasures of a fragrant garden are yours to explore. But remember: Take the time to reflect on what you want before you plant.

THE SECRET GARDEN

Sitting on the front porch is not as popular as it once was. More desirable today, it seems, is a tranquil and perhaps secluded spot as a refuge from our chaotic and fast-paced lives. A well-kept and private place in the garden becomes an outdoor room in which to read or rest, a retreat that grows in beauty and form each year. Concealing even a small part of the garden has the effect of making it feel larger and more complex. A change like this takes little money, and makes a great contribution to your peace and contentment. This is where vines come in.

As you introduce privacy to the garden, or to a portion of it, you make mystery and surprise possible. Even in a small yard, a square in the corner can be given over for a private area in which to read or rest. Trellises, tall enough that a standing person can't see over them, can be placed to form three sides of an enclosure. On the fourth side, an arch or entryway, perhaps fashioned from small sections of trellis on either side, will make the area inviting. The trellises become screens when covered with quick-growing, good-looking vines. They form the skeleton of the "secret garden," which may be designed in any size. What you plant here will determine whether this is an area of quiet or bright color. The trellis may be covered with ivy for a tranquil look, and the arch covered with climbing roses and clematis for cheery charm. To complete this shady haven of vines, add a seat or bench and plant green groundcovers. A formal walk or path from the house to the arch invites a stroll in that direction. This is but one dreamy idea to suggest the many possibilities while you plot and plan. Planning, as you probably well know, saves labor, time and money. It is also the way to make a truly great garden.

Trumpet vine and climbing hydrangea frame the entrance to a pool and its surrounding secret gardens.

The Garden's Timekeepers

The blossoms of moonflowers and morning glories open for only a day. However, buds form continuously and masses of flowers are produced from midsummer to frost. Moonflowers, as their name implies, open as the sun starts to set, around five o'clock, and close the next morning just after dawn. (On a cloudy day they may stay open until midmorning.) Morning glories open with the morning light; they close midday if it is hot and sunny, but will stay open all day if it is cloudy and pleasant. It is possible for those with patience to watch them open, as long as they don't turn their backs. The individual flowers puff first, so it is easy to pick out the ones that are ready to open. They begin to quiver before they open. The whole process of the opening of a moonflower takes 7 to 8 minutes, from the time they begin to quiver until they are fully open. A puffed moonflower may be picked and put in water to open indoors. If you'd like to catch the show, check the vine frequently, starting around five o'clock, to see if there is any activity. Once you find out what time they open, you can invite prompt friends for the next day's show. The process won't vary much from day to day, unless the weather is dark, overcast and nasty, in which case they might not open. For those who rise at dawn, it is possible to watch morning glories open. Botanists debate what causes the flowers to open when they do. Most believe it is triggered by the amount of, or lack of light.

In fall, the fiery foliage of Boston ivy sets the landscape ablaze.

COLORFUL FOLIAGE

Green is the most restful of all colors. It is the gardener's favorite color, and a greener world is his or her goal. Vines grown only for the color of their foliage add a lushness, as well as a more peaceful mood, to many a city building. Ivy is the usual choice, but Dutchman's pipe with its large, heart-shaped leaves can be equally inviting. Some vines such as porcelain vine, *Eunonymus fortunei* and *Hedera helix* grow with plain green leaves, or with variegated leaves with a silvery white luster that give the impression of newly fallen snow in summer. By contrast, the golden hops, gold-net honeysuckle and 'Goldheart' ivy add a bit of sunshine wherever they are planted.

The blossoms of morning glories open with the midmorning sun and close as evening approaches. Each flower lasts only a day, but buds form continuously, and masses of flowers are produced from midsummer until after frost.

Some uniquely colored vines may or may not be beautiful, but they certainly are attention grabbers. The kolomikta vine, of which one garden writer says has leaves that "look as if they have been dipped first in whitewash and then in raspberry juice," is one of the strangest. The leaves of *Ipomoea batatas* 'Blackie' are such a dark purple they are indeed almost black, and hyacinth bean's wine red veins give it a burgundy cast.

Whether you choose an evergreen or deciduous vine, each has its advantages. The evergreen vines clothe through all the seasons, whereas many of the deciduous vines bring vivid autumn color. Boston ivy, a deciduous vine, turns bright, bold, fiery colors in fall. For fall foliage colors at their best, the Virginia creeper offers bright shades of red and holds its beautiful leaves for a long time. Climbing hydrangea and the Oriental clematis leaves turn a golden yellow.

BIRDS AND BUTTERFLIES

The loss of natural habitats, pushed back by the building boom of modern society, means the loss of wild birds, butterflies and hummingbirds as they are forced to find new locations. To entice them to stay, a property must provide nesting places, food and water. Water is the easiest of the three to add, simply done by placing a bird bath or two in the yard. The nesting places are more complicated. The taller woody vines, those with three or more branches emerging from a central stem, are perfect nesting places for birds. Several nests of finches are found in the English ivy on the sides of our house each spring; black birds, robins, wrens and thrushes also like to nest in ivy. Last year, birds' nests also appeared in two different climbing roses, and even on our porch, a hanging basket of vinca had a nest of baby peepers.

If birds are nesting in your yard, they will feast on summer's bugs—a bonus for the gardener. Vines that bear fruit, especially those with berries that hang on the vine throughout winter such as Virginia creeper, some rose, *Euonymus fortunei* and Boston ivy, provide food for birds at the hardest time of the year for them. Plant some of these, and your yard will become a year-'round safe haven for many birds.

Summer brings hummingbirds to every part of the United States. They are fascinating to watch as they flit from bloom to bloom, seemingly never at rest. They buzz above the flowers and use their long beaks to find the nectar. As flower colors go, red is especially attractive to the hummingbird. Orange and purple are scarcely less so. In a pinch, white might do. Red, trumpet-shaped flowers are the hummingbird's first choice. Nectar, buried deep in flower trumpets, is safe from rival bees and butterflies, who aren't equipped with the necessary long beaks. Some other vines favored by hummingbirds are scarlet runner bean, nasturtiums, morning glories, trumpet honeysuckles and, obviously, the hummingbird vine (*Asarina barclaina*). While primarily nectar-eaters, hummingbirds also snatch large quantities of insects and spiders from the flowers they visit.

One morning as I sat in my bright red bathrobe drinking coffee on the back porch, a hummingbird boldly nose-dived toward me. We were both startled, and we both backed up, he more dexterously than I, with wings beating a hundred miles an hour. Apparently, in my red robe, I was a splashy attraction for him. Flowers must be planted in large, conspicuous groups to attract hummingbirds, but a single mature vine covered with flowers is conspicuous enough.

Butterflies, too, flock to nectar-rich blossoms, and they too are attracted to bright colors and fragrance. They prefer a flat landing pad for a flower. The difficulty with butterflies is that, if you attract the adults, you must be respectful of and encourage the babies, the dreaded caterpillars. Passion vine is relished by the caterpillars of the fritillary butterfly (some varieties of fritillary inhabit every part of North America). You can recognize the adult by its dull orange color with blotches of black that can be seen when its wings are spread. When the wings are closed, the underside sports a checkerboard of silver, white or yellow spots edged in black. The monarch, probably the best loved of the butterflies, is one of the showiest with its brilliant

Invite birds into your garden by providing nesting places and water for them. The birds will help keep your insect population down.

Quick-growing fleece vine is pruned to hide an inexpensive railing and add a natural finish to a hillside walkway.

Morning glories are left unpruned to give a romantic and private quality to a porch.

orange wings, black margins and veins, and splatter of white dots. Some gardeners plant parsley especially for monarch caterpillars. If they find a monarch caterpillar in another part of the garden, they will move it to a parsley plant where it will happily stay, nibbling away until it is time to hibernate.

Other interesting attractions in the three-ring circus of the summer garden include the nighttime activity of Japanese honeysuckle and moonflower. They both open their flowers at night, pure white and especially fragrant, to attract night-flying moths. The fertilized honeysuckle flowers change color from white to yellow. Both white and yellow flowers are present and long-lasting on the honeysuckle vine, another of nature's mysterious quirks.

GARDEN STRUCTURES

A structure draped with vines can provide a shady area to sit under, a screen behind which to park the wheelbarrow, a focal point in the garden or a "room divider" that separates different gardens. It can be expensive to build a trellis, gazebo, arbor or screen specifically to fit the space you have in mind, but there are a variety of prefabricated hoops, ready-made arbors, arches, trellises and gazebos available in both rustic and formal designs. They are usually made from a variety of woods, metal or plastic. A plastic trellis may be too flimsy to support certain vines or to withstand high winds. Panels of cedar trellis or of another long-lasting wood, stained or treated with a wood preservative, can be stronger and longer lasting, although more expensive. You may want to consult building plans available in woodworking books for a simple, do-it-yourself garden structure.

A simple arbor, consisting of a few posts and a trellis overhead, is attractive and beautiful, as picturesque as the grape arbors of Italian restaurants.

An arbor, rustic or formal, can be constructed over a terrace to provide a fresh, green awning for a shady outdoor dining area; free-standing away from the house, it offers a shady spot to rest, read or contemplate. Placed at the beginning or end of a walk, an arbor is inviting. Note that a free-standing arbor has to be sturdy and well secured in the ground. Bury the bottom poles a minimum of 18 inches. A permanent structure can be set in cement. Wooden posts set in cement last longer; if they are placed in heavy clay, the wood quickly rots. A wood preservative helps, but cement footings are better. (They prevent rot.) If each post hole is lined with a plastic garbage bag before the cement is poured, the concrete won't lose moisture to the soil as its cures, and it won't leach alkalies into the planting bed.

I have seen vines climbing on many ingenious, homemade structures. Bob Titus, a former director of Planting Fields Arboretum on Long Island, made arches from the metal reinforcing rods used in concrete. Available

Pictured is a simple arbor made from metal reinforcing rods and covered with the annual vines of morning glories, love-in-a-puff and hummingbird vine.

A wooden structure, densely covered with variegated ivy, creates a cool, shady place to sit.

Ready-made metal garden structures, available from many nurseries, can be placed in the garden as a sculpture for vines to cover. Pictured here is hyacinth bean.

in 20-foot lengths, they cost under 10 dollars and are easily bent. If the metal is threaded through an old green garden hose, it blends with the vines' foliage, and the rod won't rust either. The ends of the arch are fitted into larger metal pipe sunk 18 inches into the ground. When densely covered with vines, this arch is strong, yet invisible. Arches like these can be placed singly at an entryway, perhaps at the start of a path, or at the end of a path with a garden seat, a fountain or a sculpture under it. If two, three or more arches are placed in a series, they make a shady passage way.

The artist Robert Dash uses PVC (polyvinyl chloride) pipe, plastic that bends easily into arches. It is strong enough for clematis and many of the annual vines. Dash has crisscrossed two arches of pipe at the intersection of two paths at the center of his vegetable garden. The arches overlap their peaks, 8 or 9 feet high, creating four 90° angles. The angles could be adjusted if the arches were to be placed over a bench or a single path. Either

way, the arches form a dome, an effective focal point. Dash paints his arches bright colors with outdoor paint; he changes the color whenever he changes the vines.

I'm fond of arches myself. In our combined vegetable and cutting flower garden, we placed a series of three arches at the entrance between the raised beds, and covered them with various annual vines. The vines grow together, flinging their arms from one arch to the next. This archway gives the garden distinction, and the vines add to its beauty. The combination of annual vines here includes love-in-a-puff, hummingbird vine, hyacinth bean, sweet peas and morning glories. As we watched them grow, we learned how each behaved, and were eager to see which would reach the top first, which would bloom first, and which would bloom the longest. The sweet pea, which was started indoors, bloomed first but also faded first with the onset of hot weather. The love-in-a-puff, an early bloomer, reached the top first but was

quickly surpassed by the morning glory and hyacinth bean. The morning glory and hummingbird vine bloomed at about the same time, midsummer, although the hummingbird vine never reached the top of the arch. The hyacinth bean started out behind, but quickly caught up, passed over the others and bloomed well past frost. A combination of vines such as this will work well on any of the larger garden structures.

For a decorative backdrop of vines, or to frame a view, erect a series of posts 6 or more feet apart. Connect the posts with overhead arches of metal strips, 1 to 2 inches wide. Vines will grow up the posts and along the

The artist Robert Dash likes color straight from the tube for his garden structures. Ivy grows over his shed.

Formal arbors, such as this one covered with wisteria at Old Westbury Garden on Long Island, evoke the romance of another era.

semicircles of metal to connect in the center of each scallop. For more privacy, perhaps to hide the mulch pile and work area, or to divide the garden into separate rooms, the posts can be placed closer together and connected by latticework, with or without the scalloped top. Depending on the vine chosen, the screen can offer a peek-a-boo from one area to another, or it may be densely covered, as private as a solid wall.

Any garden structure deserves careful consideration and coordination of its color, the color of the contemplated vines, and the color of any visible buildings or furniture. Before you select a color, decide on the purpose of the structure and what its most important feature will be. If a trellis or gazebo is painted bright white, one of the most often used colors, it draws attention to itself, and the climbing vines become secondary. A white structure should be perfectly crafted; white highlights any design flaws. A dark or "park" green structure becomes less important, more harmonious with its surroundings. Dark green was Monet's favorite color for painted structures in his garden. A weathered or gray structure can be quaint and unobtrusive with flowering vines to dress it. Bright primary colors, colors with a straight-from-the-tube intensity, are a favorite for structures in artist Robert Dash's garden; they add humor, fun and wit, and they invariably surprise the first-time guest. So don't be timid—have a little fun with color.

VINES AS STANDARDS

For a standard, you can train a floppy vine into a tree shape with a single tall stem, or a trunk branching into a ball shape at the top. Making a standard is a process that calls for patience, especially when a plant's normal inclination is to assume a rangy, sprawling habit. Training a wisteria or an allamanda as a standard is neither difficult nor time consuming, but it does take regular checking. Wisteria is one of the vines most commonly trained as a standard, although standards are possible even with

At Wave Hill, standards of Allamanda *are focal points in the long mixed border.*

vines as flexible as ivy. To train a wisteria into a standard, start with a young vine and only allow one stem to grow. Place a strong stake the height of your intended standard's trunk, in the ground or pot next to the vine. Tie the vine loosely to the stake in several places. As the vine grows in girth, check periodically whether the top is too heavy for the stem to support. If so, pinch back the branches; this will also encourage a full ball of foliage on top. Remove any branches that sprout on the bottom two-thirds of the stem. Winter-prune back one-third of the shapely, balanced head each year to force the wisteria to bloom more abundantly.

VINE TOPIARIES

Topiary, as defined in *Hortus*, is the sculpting, through pruning, of shrubs into geometrical shapes or whimsical animal subjects. However, mock topiary can be quicker, easier and even portable. For mock topiary, thin metal wire frames in shapes are covered with quick-growing, small leaved vines. Here it's the frame, rather than the branches of the shrub, that forms the backbone of the sculpture. Sometimes a frame is placed on top of a container, and the vine planted in the container grows up and over the frame. Other times the frame is stuffed with soil and sphagnum moss and planted in various spots with plugs (small plants) of ivy, creeping fig or another small-leaved trailing or climbing plant. The vines are held in place with U-shaped

Variegated ivy grows up and over metal-wire frames in tree shapes at the formal entrance to a garden.

pins, unless they are uncooperative, in which case they are clipped. Wire wreaths, wire baskets and wire animal shapes such as rabbits, poodles and turtles are available at craft shops. Sometimes a mixture of plants is used to convey different effects. A spider plant, for example, might be used for a lion's mane. For more information, consult *The Complete Book of Topiary* by Gallup and Reich.

ESPALIER

An espalier is any shrub, tree or vine trained in an open, flat, virtually two-dimensional pattern, formal or informal, against a vertical surface. The design becomes a living architectural effect. Take a look at the *Trachelospermum* plant portrait, page 76, for a nice example of this. It is easier to produce with vines than with trees or shrubs. For a vine espalier, the side shoots are trained to "float" across the vertical surface in a pattern. Espaliered vines are trained and pruned into swags, ropes and garlands. Depending on how you cut vines, you can create a soft, fluid line or a hard-edged, geometric shape. Geometric patterns are the most popular, with diamond shapes leading the way. A geometric pattern is not difficult to achieve if the pattern is first designed over the surface with wires; the vines are then trained to follow the design. Over time, as the vines become established, regular pruning is required, often monthly.

VINES IN CONTAINERS

Vinca major _softens the hard edges of a window box as its white-edged, light green leaves contrast with both the dark green ivy and the window box itself. Red geraniums add a jolt of color._

Vines can visually tie together many different plants in one container. Probably the most popular and versatile vines for containers are vinca and ivy. As companions to enhance flowering plants in large containers or window boxes, they are hard to beat.

Grown from seed to flower within a season, annual vines reach their mature heights in a very short time. Black-eyed Susan vine, for example, is a lively climber for a hanging basket, with its arrowhead-shaped leaves and soft yellow, white, or orange daisy flowers from which round, dark, unblinking eyes peek out. It will grow up and twine around the wires that suspend a hanging basket, reaching for the ceiling, while at the same time, gallantly sweeping down to hide the basket's bare bottom. It quickly grows 5- to 6-foot-long stems, blooming as early as 60

Highlights in the History of Ivy

Ivy, the mother of vines, has been around about as long as anything that grows. Archeologists have found evidence that ivy was gathered by men as winter fodder for the earliest domesticated animals some 5,000 years ago. Early on it honored the world's great statesmen. Leaders in classical Roman times wore wreathes of ivy. Ivy was also a symbol of intellectual achievement. In those early days, even the gods wore ivy.

In the words of Lord Byron, ivy is awarded fabulous history: "... with two thousand years of ivy, grown _around an ancient tower."_

Ivy's earliest academic history, however, has its roots in England (where it also picked up a bit of whimsy). At respected Magdalen College, Oxford University, the tale is told of a strand of ivy growing up a wall. It found a crack into the cellar, and in the cellar a bottle of vintage port the learned professors had hidden away to await an appropriate occasion. The invasive ivy forced the cork into the bottle and replaced its contents with a mass of ivy roots. You can't accuse ivy of being a tasteless plant. _The popular ivy gained a reputation early. Pliny referred to it as a preventive for drunkenness and also as a cure for hangovers. It seems you can have it both ways. The result: total sobriety._

In early days ivy was thought to be medicinal, too. It was widely used as a purgative and at one time or another has been thought good for rheumatism, arthritis, fever, bruises, rashes and burns, as well as hemorrhoids. Today its chemical value is more humble. It is used mainly as a cosmetics additive.

Ivy was long a choice _of artists, its beauty displayed on vases and bowls since early civilization. Wall paintings around 2,000 B.C. show ivy with its fruit being harvested._

And finally, thanks to research at NASA, ivy has been shown to be a contributor to your good health. Hedera helix, English ivy, the most common form of ivy grown (often as a house plant) destroys benzene, a carcinogenic present in paints, solvents and cigarette smoke. It purifies the air you breathe. So, ivy is truly an all-purpose vine: practical, beautiful and thoughtful.

This container is planted to overflowing, with Mandevilla growing up a pole and geraniums and ivy spilling down.

ground and allowed to spill over the edges and down to the floor. Tropical vines, among them passion flower, bougainvillea and mandevilla, are slower growing still, but they flower all summer and can be wintered over in a sunny, south-facing window.

days from sowing. It has a mind of its own, and doesn't like to be pruned or shaped while it is blooming. So let it wander as it will, and make room for its long stems.

Morning glories, moonflowers and canary creeper, though slower to mature, are not complicated to grow. Start the seeds indoors in a peat pot, and then plant it—peat pot and all—into a larger container without disturbing the vine's roots, when its roots have filled the peat pot; don't set it out until after all danger of frost. The vines in their pots can then be placed next to an existing structure to climb on, such as a railing, banister, drain pipe or post. Or, they can be placed on a table or pedestal 4 or more feet above the

On Jack Lenor Larson's terrace, a variegated morning glory is attractive even before it reaches blooming size.

Vines for Containers

COMMON NAMES	LATIN NAMES
Allamanda	*Allamanda cathartica*
Baby winter creeper	*Euonymus fortunei* 'Minima'
Balloon vine	*Cardiospermum halicacabum*
Black-eyed Susan vine	*Thunbergia alata*
Bleeding heart vine	*Clerodendrum thomsoniae*
Bougainvillea	*Bougainvillea glabra*
Clematis	*Clematis* hybrids
Cup-and-saucer vine	*Cobaea scandens*
Dipladenia	*Mandevilla sanderi*
English ivy	*Hedera helix*
Hyacinth bean	*Dolichos lablab*
Jasmine	*Jasmine* species
Jasmine	*Jasminum polyanthus*
Moonflower	*Ipomoea alba*
Morning glory	*Ipomoea purpurea*
Nasturtium	*Tropaeolum majus*
Passionflower	*Passiflora* species
Porcelain berry	*Ampelopsis brevipedunculata* 'Elegans'
Scarlet runner bean	*Phaseolus coccineus*
Sweet pea	*Lathyrus odoratus*
Variegated Algerian ivy	*Hedera canariensis* 'Variegata'

THE VINE PLANTING AND GROWING GUIDE

MATCH THE VINE WITH THE SITE

When analyzing a site for planting a vine, there are four things to consider: the amount of available sunshine, the soil's drainage, the air circulation, and the roots of nearby trees and shrubs or the footings of a wall or house. There are vines happy in sun, part shade and shade. You have to make sure the proposed vine will have its needs met by the site.

Poor drainage is the chief obstacle for most poorly grown plants, vines included. If you suspect a drainage problem, run a test. Dig a hole on the site 18 inches deep, fill in with water and note how long it takes to empty. If water remains in the hole 6 hours later, it is necessary to improve the drainage before planting a vine. Add gypsum to lighten clay soil; it breaks apart the soil particles, for better drainage and better oxygenation. Gypsum adds calcium to the soil, enhancing root growth while it improves drainage. Peat moss and compost should be added as well, to help absorb excess water. In extremely wet areas it may be necessary to forget planting entirely, or bury drainage pipes two feet deep to conduct excess water to another part of the garden and prevent back-up water from drowning the vines.

Good air circulation is important. Puppy winds will deter mildew and fungus from attacking your vine, but too much wind might whip the vine against its support, leaving it battered and unsightly. A windy situation is not for the tender. A sturdy vine with a woody trunk or aggressive clinging abilities will fare better in windblown areas. Never plant close to a solid wall, whether it be the side of a house or a free-standing wall. The soil next to the house is the driest, especially if there are cement foundations, because they absorb moisture. Planting under an overhanging roof can be disastrous, as rain water is unlikely to reach the vine's roots. The opposite problem, too much water, could develop if the vine is planted next to a drain pipe running down from the eaves. Always plant a foot and a half or more from a solid wall, and train the vine back to the wall with a cane or wire. The perfect site is rare, but you can do much by understanding your site before you plant and addressing potential problems. The next step is to select vines that like the conditions you can't change.

At the back of a window box, a trellis supports a clematis vine. In the window box, white lilies bloom with black-eyed Susans, pink cosmos, loosestrife and miniature roses.

PREPARING THE GROUND

A vine well-planted is on its way to being well grown. As many a perennial vine will outlive its planter, soil preparation is not a good area for short cuts. Good soil preparation will make the difference between a healthy vine and a vine susceptible to disease. The old saying, "Put a dollar plant in a 10-dollar hole, not a 10-dollar plant in a dollar hole," highlights the most important point to remember; your garden can be only as good as your soil.

So when starting a garden, your greatest effort should be spent on improving your soil. Plants live and breathe; they need food, water and air. The ideal soil has good drainage, good water retention and adequate nutrients. The soil has to hold just enough water to meet the needs of the plant, but not too much, or it will force air out of the soil and deprive the plant of one of its basic needs.

Adding organic matter such as compost, leaf mulch or peat moss improves the tilth of the soil, holds air, attracts earthworms and creates an ideal condition for the bacteria that break down soil nutrients into a usable form for the plants. Keep in mind that soil amendment is not an immediate fix, but will take time to break down in the soil. Over time adding peat moss or compost will lower the pH. Ideally the pH should be between 6.0 and 6.8. A soil too alkaline or too acidic inhibits the plant's ability to use the nutrients in the soil. The addition of 5 pounds of ground limestone per 100 square feet of garden will raise the pH one point. To lower the pH from ½ to 1 point, add 3 pounds of iron sulfate or ½ pound of ground sulfur per 100 square feet of garden.

When planting a vine, dig a hole a minimum of 24 inches deep, deeper if the vine has a large root ball, and several inches wider than the circumference of the roots or root ball. If planting a cutting or a small vine, prepare the hole a foot to a foot and a half wide, in order to prepare nutritious soil for the vine's roots to grow into; the hole should be large enough for the planted vine to be surrounded on all sides by well-supplemented, nutritious soil. Depending on your type of soil and the degree of previous preparation, you may add approximately one-half to equal amounts of a mix of compost, peat moss and/or well-rotted manure to the soil removed from the hole. All three additives will improve the structure of the soil, and manure and compost add nutrients. At the very least, purchase dried cow manure and peat moss from a nursery, especially if you are preparing this hole for a lifetime of growth, as in the case of clematis (capable of living 80 years or more) or other perennials; they need the best possible start. It is ideal to place 2 inches of compost in the bottom of the hole. For bare-root vines, mound soil in the hole into an inverted cone to support the roots and help them adapt to their new conditions.

Place the potted vine in the hole, pot and all, before planting, to make sure the hole is wide and deep enough. Only then is the vine removed from the pot. Gently release the roots from the potting mixture to help them grow out into the new soil and not wind around into themselves. The roots, soil and all, are placed in the hole so that the stem will be planted at the same level it was in the pot, except in the case of clematis. Clematis should be planted 2 to 3 inches below ground level. The stem of the clematis will grow additional roots, a precaution in case the vine is struck by clematis wilt (see page 47); the buried stem will send up new shoots, and the vine will only be delayed a bit in its growth.

Fill in the hole with the remaining soil and add a slow-release fertilizer. Firm the plant in place by gently stepping around it. Mound a rim of soil 6 to 8 inches high around the edge of the hole to hold water. Water with a gentle trickle until the hole is full and water starts to run down the sides. It is important to always water new vines at the time of planting. After the vine has been well watered, and while the ground is still wet, add a mulch.

Mulching

Vines prefer their heads in the sun and their roots in shade. Mulch is an important factor in providing a happy home for any vine. Mulch conserves moisture while protecting the vine's roots from the high heat of summer. A 2- to 4-inch cover of pine needles, shredded leaves, compost, or gravel or a large stone will keep the ground moist and cool, protecting the vine's roots while inhibiting weeds. One of the best benefits of an organic mulch is that it provides nutrition as it breaks down. Rainwater will leach the nutrients from the surface through the soil to the roots.

This arbor is made from arches of reinforced rods covered with old green garden hose. Wispy branches are tied to the arches to help annual vines climb.

Fertilizers

Chemical fertilizers come in granular forms that break down quickly, in fact too quickly at times, and the nitrogen is leached with the rain water to pollute our groundwater. When adding a commercial fertilizer, it is best to use a slow-release formula that will break down over time and stay at the top of the soil. Organic fertilizers are best, returning natural ingredients to the soil. Each package of fertilizer is labeled with a code of three numbers that indicate the percentages of the 3 active ingredients in the mixture. Thus, a "5-10-5" means the fertilizer mixture contains 5% nitrogen, 10% phosphorous and 5% potassium. The remainder of the mixture is a neutral base that helps distribute the nutrients evenly. The most useful, all-around fertilizer for vines is 5-10-5. Apply it evenly and work it into the soil a week before planting time, if possible; otherwise, sprinkle it on top and water it in. Apply yearly.

For an added boost, you can liquid fertilize when transplanting and again right before flower buds open. A liquid fertilizer, if watered in deeply, goes directly to the plant roots in a form easier for the plant to absorb. However, it doesn't stay in the soil long. If your plants appear to be growing too slowly, or if they come under attack by pests or diseases, a quicker method of absorption is to use a liquid foliage feed. Use any all-purpose liquid fertilizer at half strength. It's sprayed directly on the leaves and absorbed immediately. The plant leaves themselves send the nutrition to the roots, and increase vigor. Caution: Overfeeding encourages too much foliage at the expense of flowers. Also, keep powdered fertilizers away from stems, leaves and roots, as they can burn the plant.

TO PRUNE OR NOT TO PRUNE

There are no hard-and-fast rules when it comes to pruning, only common sense. Dead stems are the only ones all gardeners agree need removing. One gardener might prune clematis yearly, and another, never. What matters is available space in the garden (an unpruned vine covers a larger area), and the shape the gardener wants the vine to take (which may differ from the willful vine's natural inclination). Pruning is sometimes an act of love for a gardener not unlike raising children. A gardener prunes to teach vines manners

A clematis grows up to and under an awning to decorate a store window with its seedpods.

and keep them from being unruly; discipline must be enforced. It is especially important to prune regularly the "movers and shakers," fast-growing vines with the ability to smother or strangle other plants, or even maim buildings, lifting tiles and pulling out mortar. Clipped and disciplined, such vines can grow up to be model citizens. Some slow-growing vines may not need to be pruned at all. If a vine is trained to climb a tree, for example, it is almost impossible and not really necessary to prune it. For the individual pruning needs of a particular vine, refer to the plant portraits (page 37).

When to Prune

1. Prune to improve a vine's appearance, for example, when a spindly branch or a stem growing in the wrong direction needs correction, or if the vine becomes a tangled mess.
2. Prune to keep the vine confined to the allotted space. Vines growing on buildings will have to be pruned to keep them from covering windows and doors.
3. Prune flowers that bloom on new growth in winter or early spring to encourage the most flowers. If these vines are not pruned, the flowers will bloom higher on the vine, which may or may not be what you want.
4. Prune vines that bloom on the previous year's growth as soon as they finish flowering, to allow them to grow stems for the next year's flowers, unless the flowers will form decorative fruit, berries or seed pods. In cases such as these, you have to choose what you will lose.
5. Prune out dead stems for both the appearance and health of the vine. Pruning out a dead, diseased stem may help prevent the disease from spreading.
6. Weak, broken or diseased shoots should be removed as soon as they are noticed.

Whenever you prune, do it carefully, stepping back frequently to see how the vine looks. Too often, a hurried pruning ends up like a bad haircut, lopsided and too short. Use only sharp pruners and make a clean cut. Diseases and fungus enter more easily through torn and raggedly cut stems.

Some "Movers and Shakers"

COMMON NAMES	LATIN NAMES
Bittersweet	*Celastrus* species
Creeping fig	*Ficus pumila*
Fiveleaf akebia	*Akebia quinata*
Fleece vine	*Polygonum aubertii*
Honeysuckle	*Lonicera japonica*
Hops	*Humulus* species
Ivy	*Hedera helix*
Kudu	*Pueraria lobata*
Poison ivy	*Rhus radicans*
Porcelain vine	*Ampelopsis brevipedunculata*
Trumpet vine	*Campsis* species
Virginia creeper	*Parthenocissus quinquefolia*
Wisteria	*Wisteria* species

In Kay Reeves' garden, a potted mandevilla summers outdoors next to an evergreen shrub, which it uses instead of a trellis.

LAYERING

The simplest and surest way to propagate most established perennial vines is by layering. In layering, a portion of stem is induced to root while the stem is still connected to and nourished by the mother plant. This requires tender stems with the flexibility to bend to the ground to allow a few inches of the stem, approximately a foot from the end, to be buried a few inches underground. To layer, fill a 5- to 8-inch flowerpot with good compost or a potting mix. Choose an area of stem of your vine above a bud eye, and carefully scrape off an inch-long strip of the outer layer or bark, exposing the pith. Bury the pot a few inches under the part of the stem to be induced to root. Coat the pith on the underside of the stem with rooting hormone and bury it "face down" a few inches at the center of the pot. Where the stem has been scraped is where the roots of the new vine will grow. It is usually necessary to place a rock on top of the stem to hold it down. The layering process takes a year or more before the roots are strong enough for the baby to be severed from the mother plant.

The buried pot protects the new roots from being disturbed or hurt when the new vine with its fragile root system is transplanted to another spot.

PROPAGATION THROUGH CUTTINGS

Some vines that are slow to grow from seed are readily propagated through cuttings. Depending on the type of vine, cuttings can be taken at different times of the year. Fall is the time to take cuttings from annual vines to grow indoors over the winter and plant outdoors again in spring, or to use as houseplants. Spring or summer is the right time for many perennial vines.

To propagate from cuttings:

1. Cut a 3- to 4-inch piece of a new, tender stem; make sure to cut ½ inch below a node, the place where two or more branches or leaves come together. This is essential, as the cutting will then have sufficient food reserves within its tissues to sustain it until roots have been produced. (Clematis are an exception as they will root from any part of the stem and don't need a heel or node at the bottom of the cutting for rooting. Instead, a short piece of stem underneath a pair of leaves with one of the leaves removed will do. The Montana varieties are the easiest, rooting in 4 to 6 weeks. Large-flowered hybrids take longer and are less sure; commercial propagators use cuttings from one-year-old plants grown in greenhouses because cuttings from older, outdoor vines tend to be too hard and take too long for easy rooting. Still, for the patient home gardener who uses a little hormone powder, they may root in time.)

2. Retain two sets of leaves, to prevent wilting and to promote rooting; more than two sets makes it hard for the stem to stay alive without roots. Remove any flowers or flower buds to prevent them from sapping the stem's energy. Most cuttings benefit from being dipped in a rooting hormone, which helps speed the growth of healthy new roots.

3. Fill a tray or a cup with moist, not soggy, rooting medium (sand and vermiculite are two). Make a hole in the medium using a pencil. This hole should be wider than the stem, so the stem doesn't lose any of the hormone powder clinging to it when it is placed in the medium. Stand the stem up in the hole and gently push the rooting medium around it. Place the node under the medium; this is where the roots will form.

4. Cover the pot loosely with clear plastic or put it in a plastic bag, and place in a warm spot. This will keep the atmosphere moist. Rooting is promoted by moisture and warmth, particularly bottom heat. Use the top of a refrigerator, a warm (not hot) radiator or a cold frame in partial sun. Do not place the pot in full sun, which will burn the cutting. Add water if the pot seems dry; vent the plastic covering briefly if it is too wet.

5. Different plants root at different speeds, and as long as your stems look healthy, they are probably fine. If you detect rot or mildew, separate the stem from other cuttings and discard it.

6. You will know the plant has developed roots when new growth has begun, or when a gentle tug on the stem meets with resistance. It takes a month or longer for roots to develop.

COMPOSTING

A garden is only as good as its soil. Composting and a yearly replenishing of the nutrients in the soil are the most important steps a gardener can take toward building a beautiful garden. Without nutrients, plants won't grow. Nature, however, makes it easy. All the gardener needs to do is follow her lead and work with her. A simple pile of leaves left behind the garage to decompose becomes perfectly adequate compost. The leaves will break down over the year into a fine, black humus, which can be shovelled onto the garden each fall. The nutrients in the compost will be carried through the soil to the plants' roots by rainwater and will be readily available in the spring when needed.

Once you see the results of adding compost to your garden, you will not be willing to wait a year for leaves to break down. There are almost as many different methods of composting as there are gardeners. The purpose of each of the different methods is to speed up nature's decomposition. A pile left standing behind the garage to decompose on its own is the slowest method of producing compost. If leaves are layered in a compost bin, alternated with an inch of soil, a sprinkling of ground limestone, and watered thoroughly, the many organisms in the soil will help break the leaves down faster. Decomposition can be further speeded up if the pile is turned over every week or two. There are also ready-made compost bins available that keep in heat and further speed the process.

My preference is to rake leaves in fall and shred them on the spot, returning them directly to the garden. Shredded leaves are attractive as a mulch; they give the plants some winter protection and provide nutrients in the spring because they break down quickly. By shredding them on the spot, I eliminate the steps of bagging and moving the leaves and carrying them back to the garden in summer. I do keep a compost pile for garden clean-up that is filled with excess leaves, vegetable peelings, grass clippings and other material gathered over the entire year, not just in the fall.

What goes in the compost pile:

Remember that the smaller the pieces are, the faster they will decompose:

♦ *Shredded or whole fall leaves (drag a lawn mower back and forth over leaves to shred or use a leaf shredder)*
♦ *Shredded bark (you'll need a wood chipper for this)*
♦ *Shredded twigs*
♦ *Fresh vegetable and fruit peelings*
♦ *Grass cuttings*
♦ *Tea leaves*
♦ *Coffee grounds*
♦ *Well-rotted horse or cow manure*

♦ *Eggshells*
♦ *Cut flowers*
♦ *Salt hay**
♦ *Pine needles*

What not to put in the compost pile:

♦ *Cooked food*
♦ *Weeds with seedpods*
♦ *Raw fish and animal remains (good compost, but they attract mice and other small animals)*
♦ *Diseased plants (the disease will spread)*
♦ *Any plant material that has been treated with a herbicide or pesticide within the past three weeks*

*This is made from wild grass (sold at nurseries) grown in salt water. Unlike common hay, salt hay does not contain seeds.

This compost starter bin is easy to make from four 4-foot posts, set in a rectangle, wrapped in chicken wire. If the chicken wire is secured loosely on the fourth side, the bin can be opened easily for removal of compost or for working the compost pile.

Children's Teepee Garden

A tepee covered with vines is a favorite place for Katie Bales to play.

A colorful, easy-to-grow, vine-covered tepee will provide children with countless imaginative summer activities. Imagine their delight watching vines climb up the teepee poles, creating a special place for them to hide and play. Choose fast-growing vines (morning glory, moonflower, love-in-a-puff, Jack-be-little pumpkin and scarlet runner bean, to list a few), so children can enjoy watching them grow day by day. Seeds sown directly in the garden where they are to grow are easiest for children to plant. Scarlet runner bean or a favorite pea or bean vine offers children the dividend of being able to reach out and nibble a young bean pod while they play in the teepee.

The teepee can be grown in the middle of a vegetable garden, an area of lawn or to one side of a children's play area. Choose a location with good drainage that receives at least 6 hours of sun a day. Prepare 5 or 6 small plots, each approximately 1 foot square, around the outside of the teepee, one plot for each pole the vines are to climb. Work in organic material such as compost or peat moss. Follow the directions on the seed packs for planting and growing. Plant several seeds in each prepared plot to assure at least one will germinate and grow. Water with a fine spray to prevent the newly planted seeds from washing away. Keep the soil moist until the plants have emerged (7 to 21 days, depending on the type of vine, soil and weather conditions) and are well established. When the seedlings are large enough to handle, thin them out but to closer spacing than recommended for each variety on the seed packets. As the vines mature, you can prolong the harvest and increase the production by regularly picking the dead flowers or beans. Lawn can be left to grow inside the circle, but it will need to be clipped by hand. It will be in deep shade only at the end of the summer; after the teepee is removed, the grass will grow back.

VINE PORTRAITS

The vines described in this chapter were chosen for their popularity, easy culture and availability. They are grown for their beautiful flowers, their fragrance or their decorative—although usually not edible—fruit. Almost all the vines included have beautiful foliage, and for some, that is their special claim to fame. (Climbing vegetables can be decorative, and they are discussed in Burpee American Gardening Series: *Vegetables*.) As vines vary from the quick growing to the slow, the tall to the short, the perennial to the annual, you'll have an abundance of choices to make. The warmer your climate, the more vines you'll have to choose from. Still, there are so many choices that whatever your needs and wherever you live, there are many vines that will please you.

The vines are listed under their botanical (Latin) names, and cross-referenced by their common names. Having the plant information you want listed under the scientifically correct name avoids confusion, because many plants have the same common name. The system of botanical nomenclature, founded by the Swedish botanist Carolus Linnaeus, gives every known plant a first name, the genus (indicated by the first Latin word), which is a grouping of plants with similar characteristics. Every plant has a second Latin name, too, the species, which further identifies shared qualities of lesser importance; you'll notice many vines have the second Latin name *scandens*, which translates to mean climbing or growing upward. Although common names are easier to pronounce, they can be misleading because many vines grown in different parts of the country under the same common name are in fact from different families. For example, there are several vines with the common name of jasmine. Winter jasmine and scented star jasmine have the Latin name of *Jasminum*, while Madagascar jasmine is *Stephanotis*, Carolina jasmine is *Gelsemium* and yellow star jasmine is *Trachelospermum*. Using botanical names is the one way to be sure of having the correct cultural information.

PLANT PORTRAIT KEY

Here is a guide to the symbols and terms used throughout this section:

Latin name of the vine is in boldface italic type.
Phonetic pronunciation of the Latin name is in parentheses.
Common name of the vine is in boldface type.
Symbols for other important characteristics are as follows:

F	*Fragrant blooms or leaves*
A	*Annual*
TP	*Tender perennial*
P	*Perennial*
D	*Deciduous*
E	*Evergreen*
SE	*Semievergreen*
NA	*Native American*
CF	*Cut flowers*

In Robert Dash's garden the scarlet runner bean in the foreground will completely cover the wire fence by summer's end. The trumpet vine in the background will attract hummingbirds.

Actinidia kolomikta's spring foliage is tipped with pink and white.

The average hours of sun needed per day are indicated by symbols. The first symbol is what the vine prefers, but the vine is adaptable to all conditions listed.

○ *Sun* — Six or more hours of strong, direct sunlight per day

◑ *Part shade* — Three to six hours of direct sunlight per day

● *Shade* — Two hours or less of direct sunlight

Heights are for normal growth, but vines with fertile soil and a longer growing season could grow taller. Conversely, with poor growing conditions, the plant could be shorter.

Zones for best growth. Check the USDA plant hardiness map (pages 90–91), based on average annual temperatures for each area—or USDA zone—of the United States to see what zone you live in. Some vines will grow better in northern gardens (Zones 3 through 7), some better in southern gardens (Zones 8 through 10), and a few will grow anywhere. We have listed which zones are best for each vine, although there is room for error. A protected corner of a garden in Zone 6, for example, might be in a microclimate closer to that of Zone 7, thereby extending the gardener's choices. Don't be afraid to experiment occasionally with plants that grow in a zone one removed from yours, especially if you provide some winter protection.

Cultural information explains the vines' preferences and provides information on how best to grow them.

Actinidia (ak-tin-ID-ia) *Actinidia kolomikta*, kolomikta vine, P, F, D, ○ ◑

Zones: 4 to 10
Height: 15 to 20 feet
Colors: Green, white and pink foliage; white flowers
Characteristics: Few vines can rival kolomikta for spring foliage color when the heart-shaped leaves, up to 5 inches long, first open purple, then soften to a striking combination of lime green splashed with pink and white, and occasionally red. With the approach of summer the leaves lose their variegation, remaining a lime green throughout the summer. Their stems are a colorful brownish red. Their spring coloration improves each year as the vine ages, and is more pronounced in full sun. In May and June kolomikta bears lightly fragrant clusters of small, ½- to ¾-inch-wide, white flowers with yellow anthers. Greenish-yellow fruit, oval and 1 inch long, are produced on female plants when a male plant is nearby to provide the pollen. One of the more exuberant, though slim, vines, kolomikta grows to 20 feet (occasionally more) and needs strong supports. This native of northern India, China and Japan climbs by twining. Although kolomikta vines are deciduous, they are useful for covering walls, fences, arches, arbors and porches.
Cultural Information: Kolomikta are not difficult to grow and readily adapt to a wide range of conditions. They prefer a moist but well-drained soil, and need frequent watering in hot, dry weather. When planted in a rich soil they can become rampant. The coloration is generally better in the foliage of male plants, especially when grown in a limey soil or one rich in calcium. Prune in winter or spring to keep the vine within bounds, but remember that the vine flowers on the previous year's growth. Kolomikta can be grown from seed or cuttings. In midsummer, cuttings made from firm shoots of the current year's growth (not from woody stems) can be propagated in moist sand, and grown indoors over winter to be planted outdoors in spring. Propagation is also possible by layering the ends of trailing branches.

Akebia (ak-EE-bee-a) *Akebia quinata*, five-leaf akebia, chocolate vine, P, F, D, ○ ◑ ●

Zones: 4 to 10
Height: Up to 40 feet
Color: Purple
Characteristics: Jack's bean stalk could have reached the clouds about as quickly if he had planted akebia instead of beans. It grows vigorously, 15 or more feet the first year. With little care, and when properly controlled, you can have a graceful twining, woody vine to train on a fence or a wall. Not a showy vine, akebia has spicy-scented flowers hidden under spring's new leaves. When you find them, the chocolate-maroon flowers are quite pretty; these are the female flowers, about 1 inch across. The small clusters of male flowers are a

Akebia quinata's *spicy scented spring flowers hide under the leaves.*

rosy-purple, ½ inch across. In fall, 2¼- to 4-inch purple-violet, sausagelike pods appear.

The open habit and lovely texture of akebia's dainty leaves, each divided into 5 leaflets, and notched at the tip, make it useful for draping over arbors or for partially hiding unsightly objects. Some gardeners even use akebia as a groundcover—it creates a billowy carpet as it spreads. However, it is important to remember that akebia is a rapid, vigorous grower and can become invasive. One winter my family purchased a house, never having seen the back yard in summer. It had a rocky terrain with what looked like a meadow, but in fact, akebia had been allowed to run rampant for decades. It dangled from the trees in the shady locations and blanketed the shrubs and meadow in the sunny areas. Up to this time I had believed akebia to be a well-behaved, easy-to-control vine. Just as different sides of people shine in different situa-

tions, so it is with plants. On my grape arbor it grows at the shady side and is quite beautiful and easy-going, but I give it a good hacking yearly. I have seen akebia growing beautifully over a trellis at the entrance to a house, where it shades a front seat on the side of an otherwise nude house. In both instances the owner trimmed some of the foliage in spring to expose the shy flowers. South of Zone 7 the vines are evergreen in mild winters. With a little more care, they can be used indoors in a cool, light place.

Akebia vines twist counterclockwise from left to right as they climb and are useful for covering trellises, porches, arbors and fences. Akebia leaves are compound, with 5 oval leaflets, yellowish green underneath, bluish green on top in summer. While the name akebia is of Japanese origin, the plant grows wild in China, Japan and Korea.

Cultural Information: Five-leaf akebia does well in moderately fertile soils and slightly acid to

neutral soils (pH 6.0–7.0), but grows in any well-drained soil. They prefer a light to a heavy soil. Select an area where the plant will receive good light, not necessarily direct sunlight. Plan for at least 2 feet between plantings. To train your vine, provide a sturdy trellis or support poles. *A. quinata* grows up to 40 feet. To keep the plants under control, prune your vine severely each fall or early spring after the flowers have bloomed. Tie in any unruly branches. Plants will recover quickly even if cut back to a foot from the ground every 3 or 4 years. Akebia tolerates wind, and is remarkably resistant to disease and insects. It can be grown from seed (germinating quickly if sown when fresh), root division, layering and stem cuttings.

Algerian ivy; see *Hedera*

Allamanda (al-a-MAN-da) ***Allamanda cathartica,* allamanda, golden trumpet vine,** TP, F, E, ○ ◑
Zone: 10
Height: Vine, 30 to 50 feet; shrub, 2 to 4 feet
Color: Yellow
Characteristics: Bring a touch of the tropics indoors with allamanda. Allamanda grows wild in Brazil but calmly adapts to indoor living. It is an exotic indoor plant, a vigorous evergreen vine with brilliant golden flaring trumpets 3 to 5 inches across, that makes itself at home on a windowsill. Grown indoors in a pot, it will be much smaller than it would be in the garden. Loose-limbed and floppy, it needs to be tied

Allamanda cathartica *is a tropical vine that will bloom for 9 months or longer even on a sunny windowsill.*

Porcelain vine lights up a shady corner with its variegated leaves and its red stems even before it is covered with colorful berries.

In spring, the small pipe-shaped flowers hide under the large leaves of Aristolochia durior, *commonly called Dutchman's pipe.*

to a sturdy support; a horizontal wire with ties 3 feet apart works well. The flowers bloom 9 or more months of the year, starting in early spring, with the most profuse bloom in summer. The foliage is deep green, glossy and waxy. Each leaf is approximately 4 inches across. The fragrance has been described as "wine after dark." If you're cutting off dead flowers to clean up the vine, remember that all parts of the plant are poisonous, including the milky sap. The vine can also be pruned into a shrub. It is tender and susceptible to cold, so it is important to give it protection at night if it is grown where frost occurs. *A cathartica* 'Williamsii' is one of the best yellow varieties, with double flowers 3 inches across. *A. violacea* is a purple allamanda with magenta-violet, bell-shaped flowers that fade to a two-toned effect; it grows best when grafted on rooted cuttings of *A. cathartica*.

Cultural Information: Grow allamanda outdoors in full sunshine or in light shade. When growing it as a houseplant, ensure a minimum of 4 hours of sunshine a day. Use a sterile potting soil and keep it moist, but not soggy. Fertilize with a half-strength liquid fertilizer every other week. The plant needs a dormant period in the winter, when it should be watered sparingly without fertilizer; the night temperatures can go as low as 55° F. When the plant is flowering, night temperatures should be above 60° F., and day temperatures 70° F. or above. Allamanda is easily propagated from root cut-

tings, 3 inches long, planted in moist sand or vermiculite. The cuttings will develop faster if they are grown with bottom heat of 75° to 80° F. These plants are rarely bothered by pests and disease.

American bittersweet; see *Celastrus*

Ampelopsis (am-pel-OP-sis) *Ampelopsis brevipedunculata,* **porcelain vine, blueberry climber, P, D, ○ ◐**
Zones: 4 to 10
Height: 20 or more feet
Color: Berries are assorted pastel colors
Characteristics: Originally from Northeast Asia, the porcelain vine resembles its cousin the grapevine in the way it holds its clusters of ¼-inch, grapelike berries, and in the shape of its leaves. But the berries, ripening in late summer, are multicolored pastels with a finish that resembles cracked glazed porcelain. The colorful mix of light green, turquoise, lavender, deep purple and pink can all be present in the same cluster. The beautiful berries attract birds. They are also a great addition to fall flower arrangements.

Porcelain vine pulls itself up by forked, twining tendrils and can grow 15 to 20 feet a year. In many areas of the country it grows freely along the roadsides and can be invasive and a nuisance. The variegated variety is less vigorous and even more beautiful; the berries are the same on both. When I glance out my window at the variegated porcelain vine draping the fence, I'd think it was

covered with summer snow if I didn't know better. Porcelain vines are useful for covering arbors, and clambering over large trees or shrubs. They are deciduous, so whatever they cover in summer will be bare in winter. *A. brevipedunculata* 'Elegans' is variegated with tones of pink and white in the leaves. It is a smaller, less vigorous vine and makes a splendid hanging basket plant.

Cultural Information: Porcelain vine prefers light soil, but it tolerates even heavy clay. Severely pruned in early spring, it can be shaped and kept in bounds. Propagate by stem cuttings, seeds, or by pegging a stem to the ground in spring and allowing it to grow roots. The new plant can be cut from the mother the following spring and planted elsewhere.

Arabian tea jasmine; see *Jasminum*

Aristolochia (a-riss-to-LO-kee-a) *Aristolochia durior,* **Dutchman's pipe, pipe vine, calico flower, P, F, D, ○ ◐ ●**
Zones: 4 to 8
Height: 20 to 30 feet
Color: Dull green
Characteristics: Dutchman's pipe has a woody stem and is grown for its decorative large, rounded heart-shaped, deep green, glossy leaves, often a foot long. They make a dense cover as they alternate along the stem in an overlapping, shingled pattern. The dull, greenish flowers, shaped like small pipes with flared bowls, have an odd, though not unpleasant, odor when they bloom in spring; for the most part they

Dutchman's pipe (Aristolochia durior) is trimmed to decorate J. Barry Ferguson's breezeway at his stable.

Asarina's individual flowers resemble snapdragons and are attractive to hummingbirds.

are hidden under the large leaves. The interior of the flower is filled with tiny hairs, all pointing downward. Insects easily enter the flower and are trapped by the hairs, which prevent them from exiting. Miraculously, after a trapped insect has feasted on the nectar, the stigma withers and the hairs relax. The insect is then allowed to leave, taking pollen with it as it heads off for another blossom to repeat the cycle; in this way the flowers are pollinated. Dutchman's pipe grows wild in California and elsewhere in the southern United States. It grows quickly and can crowd out less aggressive vines, so give it room.

Cultural Information: Growth of the vine is slow in the early years until the roots are well established. Then it takes off with rocket speed, so provide a heavy-duty trellis from the beginning for it to twist on. Once the roots are established it can be cut to the ground in spring and will quickly regrow; this can be very handy if your vine is growing on a building or trellis you would like to repaint. It requires only average soil and is rarely bothered by diseases and insects. It is easily grown from seed.

Asarina (AS-a-rina) *Asarina Antirrhiniflora; Asarina barclaina,* **maurandia, creeping glorinia, climbing snapdragon, chickabiddy, hummingbird vine,** TP, A, ○

Zones: 9 and 10
Height: 6 feet
Colors: Red and yellow, purple
Characteristics: Asarina is originally from South America, and its Latin name comes from the Spanish word for snapdragon, which the individual flowers resemble. There are a dozen or more varieties available, and they are all attractive to hummingbirds. The vine climbs by twining. It is a tender perennial that will need protection from frost if it is to survive north of Zone 9. It is grown as an annual in areas where frost occurs. *A. antirrhiniflora* has 1-inch red and yellow flowers like those of the snapdragon.

Cultural Information: Sow seeds in early February, as the seedling grow slowly at first. Germination can take 2 to 3 weeks. Set the seedlings out after all danger of frost, planting 1 foot apart. The flowers will bloom approximately 18 weeks after the seeds sprout. They will continue to bloom until heavy frost.

Balloon-vine; see ***Cardiospermum***

Bitter nightshade; see ***Solanum***

Bittersweet; see ***Solanum***

Bittersweet, American; see ***Celastrus***

Bittersweet, Oriental; see ***Celastrus***

Black-eyed Susan vine; see ***Thunbergia***

Black morning glory; see ***Ipomoea***

Black-vined sweet potato; see ***Ipomoea***

Bleeding heart vine; see ***Clerodendrom***

Blueberry climber; see ***Ampelopsis***

Blue crown passion flower; see ***Passiflora***

Boston ivy; see ***Parthenocissus tricuspidata***

Bougainvillea elegantly dresses an archway at Hearst Castle.

Bougainvillea (boo-gen-VILL-ee-a) ***Bougainvillea glabra*,** **lesser bougainvillea, paper flower;** ***Bougainvillea spectabilis*,** **bougainvillea;** ***Bougainvillea peruviana*,** **bougainvillea;** ***Bougainvillea × buttiana*,** **bougainvillea;** E, ○ ◐
Zones: 9 to 10
Height: Variable; from 3 feet in a hanging basket to more than 30 feet when planted in the ground.
Colors: White, pink, salmon, butterscotch, bronze, gold-orange, red
Characteristics: Bougainvillea in any of its bold, glowing, neon colors of flamingo pink, passionate purple, salmon, bronze, gold, and outrageous orange is a head-turner; you can't pass it without turning to stare. This is not a plant for the timid, although there is a bright white available, which becomes a soft beacon at night. Every statement bougainvillea makes is excessive. When it flowers, it puts out so many blossoms it is hard to see the leaves. The colorful part of the plant is really the papery bracts that surround the true tiny, creamy yellow flowers. Originally from Brazil, bougainvillea is now common in all southern states where it scrambles along highways, climbs arbors and brightly colors the landscape with colors that can be seen for miles in any direction. A short winter freeze in the South can kill it back to the ground, but if the vine is established it usually survives. Bougainvillea's long, arching stems lean on supports, and need to be tied to a trellis or wire framework in order to climb. It blooms best in late winter and early spring when days are short and nights cool. It produces inconspicuous little ribbed seed pods. Double-flowering cultivars tend to look messy as they hold their bracts too long after they have faded.

B. spectabilis is the rampant variety, especially recommended when there is a large area to cover as it easily grows to 30 feet. Its purple flowers keep coming even in cool summers. It can be trained as a shrub or clipped as a hedge, and it can climb walls and arbors. *B. glabra* is the best variety for growing in a pot or basket, as it blooms more when its roots are crowded. It is also often trained to grow as a small tree. 'Harrisii' is a variety with variegated leaves. Many different colors are available, and names of some of the popular varieties reflect their colors: 'Cherry Blossom', 'Jamaica White', 'Orange King', 'Pink Tiara' and 'White Madonna'.

Cultural Information: Bougainvillea's popularity stems in part from the fact that most of the time it cares for itself. It likes to dry out between waterings, and tolerates drought for brief periods. In climates that have both a dry and a wet season, the vine will lose its leaves during the dry season, but grow with added vigor and more blooms during the wet season. It prefers slightly acid soil and becomes susceptible to mineral deficiencies when grown in lime soils. Remove a vine purchased in a plastic pot with care. Unlike those of most plants, the roots of bougainvillea don't hold the soil in a pot together in a firm root ball. Their roots don't like to be disturbed, and the plant could be fatally damaged if removed by the traditional method of knocking it from the container. If the container is plastic, cut out the bottom, place the pot in the prepared hole, and only then remove the sides and fill the hole with soil.

When growing in a container, bougainvillea prefers its roots crowded and requires only a temperature of 46° to 54° F., no food, and little water while resting all winter. When nights reach 60° F. it can be moved outdoors; vines rest if the temperatures plunge below 60° F. Keep the stems pruned back to 3 or 4 feet long, to prevent the plant from producing sharp thorns. Place it in full sun daily during the summer. On hot days the vine wilts easily, but when watered its recovery is quick. It tolerates salt air and can be grown just back from sand dunes.

Calico flower; see ***Aristolochia***

Campsis (KAMP-sis) ***Campsis grandiflora*,** Chinese trumpet creeper; ***Campsis radicans*,** trumpet vine, trumpet creeper, cow-itch; ***Campsis tagliabuana* 'Madame Galen',** Madame Galen trumpet creeper; P, NA, D, ○ ◐
Zones: 4 to 9
Height: 30 to 50 feet
Colors: Yellow, orange, coral, red
Characteristics: The brightly colored, blaring trumpets of *Campsis radicans* and *C. tagliabuana* 'Madame Galen' demand attention even from a distance. Trumpet vine is a dense woody vine, wonderful for midsummer color on a porch or fence. The flowers are also a favorite with hummingbirds. *Campsis radicans,* a native of the eastern United States, is covered with brilliant orange-red, 3-inch, trumpet-shaped flowers. The flowers are borne in clusters of from 6 to 12. They have scattered blooms from the end of June to October with their most abundant bloom in July. In the fall spindle-shaped seed capsules develop, each containing many winged seeds. The compound foliage is emerald green and trouble-free. It readily attaches itself by ivylike aerial roots, or holdfasts, which cling to walls and other supports. I have seen it grown up tall trees beautifully. If grown against a building, prune to under the roof line to prevent the vine from lifting the shingles. As it gets older, it may become quite heavy and require the additional support of a trellis. Trumpet vines can be pruned to be bushy shrubs or hedges. This is a tough, durable plant that tolerates wind and part sun. If killed to the ground by a deep freeze, it will send up new shoots quickly. 'Flava' is a yellow-flowered variety of *C. radicans. C. tagliabuana* 'Madame Galen' is similar in most respects to *C. radicans* (one of its parents), but it has coral flowers that are slightly larger and grows to 25 feet. The vines are excellent for cut flowers, but note that ants frequently hide in the flowers. The ants don't bother the vines. To rid the flowers of ants, submerge them in a bucket of water before bringing them indoors. Although it rarely happens, some people develop a skin irritation and blisters from contact with the leaves and flowers.

Cultural Information: Trumpet vines prefer a fertile, moderately moist soil containing leaf mold or humus. Turn over the soil well to encourage the plant roots to spread out, and set the crown below the soil surface; avoid shallow planting. Bare-root vines should have their roots soaked in water for several hours before planting. Dig the hole twice as wide and deep as the roots. As the plants climb by aerial rootlets, it's wise to have posts or other supports in place before planting.

When planting a new vine, cut its growth back to 6 or 8 inches from the ground to encourage new shoots. Only new shoots attach themselves to supports. Trumpet vines can be propagated by stem cuttings, seed and root cuttings. In fact, if you move a trumpet vine and leave a piece of root behind in the soil, it will send up another vine. It also spreads itself with suckering roots. In warmer climates trumpet vine can be grown against a wooden building, but will have to be cut back if you want to repaint. Annual pruning to remove dead wood, and shorten and thin out branches, is best done in the early spring. The flowers bloom on young wood, so it's important not to prune indiscriminately. Established vines can be fertilized with slow-release fertilizer in spring or early summer.

Campsis radicans' *trumpet flowers are a favorite with hummingbirds.*

Growing here over a garden shed, Campsis tagliabuana *'Madame Galen' has coral trumpet flowers, slightly larger than those of its parent,* C. radicans.

When the green puffs of Cardiospermum halicacabum, love-in-a-puff, brown, three jet-black seeds marked with perfect white hearts can be found hiding inside.

Canary-bird flower; see *Tropaeolum*

Canary nasturtium; see *Tropaeolum*

Cape plumbago; see *Plumbago*

Cardinal climber; see *Ipomoea*

Cardiospermum (kar-dee-o-SPERM-um) **Cardiospermum halicacabum,** balloon vine, heart-seed, love-in-a-puff, A, ○
Height: 8 feet plus
Color: White flowers, green seed pods
Characteristics: Love-in-a-puff is a wonderful vine for introducing children to the idiosyncrasies of nature, and it's a favorite with adults who still believe in miracles. The tiny white flowers aren't much to look at; the delightful part is the 1½- to 2-inch green papery puffs, the seed pods that form continuously from midsummer until heavy frost. When the pods ripen to brown they are meant to be popped. Inside each are three jet-black seeds, each marked with a perfectly shaped, bright white heart, one of Mother Nature's delicate touches. Hence the common name of love-in-a-puff. The seeds are plentiful and easy to save for the following year. The vine's delicate and wispy limbs climb slowly, as the 1-inch tendrils curl downward like hooks. I prefer to see it twined with another vine as an added frill or decorative touch, because alone it won't attract much attention. The seeds arrived in America with the pilgrims, who used them in remedies for heart problems.
Cultural Information: Easily grown from seed, love-in-a puff will self-seed, often popping up in an unexpected place even after a cold winter. Germination can be speeded up if the seed is filed lightly with an emery board and soaked in water overnight before planting. This will soften the outer protective coating. Seed can be sown directly outdoors or started indoors in peat pots and the seedlings planted out after all danger of frost. Sow ½ inch deep. Germination takes approximately a week. Space new plants a foot to a foot and a half apart.

Cape plumbago; see *Plumbago*

Carolina jasmine; see *Gelsemium*

Cathedral bells; see *Cobaea*

Celastrus (see-LASS-trus) **Celastrus orbiculatus,** Oriental bittersweet; **Celastrus scandens,** American bittersweet; **Celastrus loeseneri;** P, D, ○ ◑ ●
Zones: C. orbiculatus, 5 to 9; C. scandens, 3 to 9
Height: C. scandens 20 feet; C. orbiculatus 30 to 40 feet
Color: Greenish-white flowers, yellow-orange and red berries
Characteristics: Bittersweet is a python of a vine, easier to control farther north where winter weather halts its growth for a season than in the South. The yellow and orange berries are a

The yellow and orange berries of bittersweet are a favorite for fall's dried arrangements. The vines are rampant growers that need a strong hand to keep them in control.

favorite for fall's dried arrangements. When the yellow papery cases burst to reveal orange-red seed, it is at its showiest. The attractive seeds are found only on the female plants; both the male and female are needed to produce them. Birds don't seem interested in the seeds, which is one reason they last into winter on the vine. Bittersweet twines as it grows. It climbs roadside trees and can shade them out or choke them to death. *Celastrus scandens,* the American variety, is the more aggressive of the two. Another available variety is *C. rosthornianus* or *C. loeseneri,* Loesener bittersweet.
Cultural Information: The problem is how to keep bittersweet in bounds, rather than how to grow it. Bittersweet thrives in sun or shade and readily adjusts to most soils, as long as they are not constantly wet. Both a male and a female plant are needed to

ensure fruit. Pruning yearly will result in more fruit and help control the vine. One problem is controlling the underground roots, which are often so invasive they produce new plants in unwanted places and crowd out others. This can be controlled by root pruning, cutting roots off with a spade.

Chickabiddy; see *Asarina*

Chilean glory vine; see *Eccremocarpus*

Chilean jasmine; see *Mandevilla*

Chinese fleece vine; see *Polygonum*

Chinese gooseberry; see *Actinidia*

Chinese trumpet creeper; see *Campsis*

Chinese wisteria; see *Wisteria*

Chocolate vine; see *Akebia*

Clematis (KLEM-a-tis) **clematis,** P, F (many varieties), D, ○ ◑
Zones: 3 to 9
Height: Large-flowered hybrids, 8 to 20 feet; small-flowered species, up to 30 feet
Colors: Pink, purple, blue, white, red, bicolor
Characteristics: In a galaxy of

Clematis × jackmanii *is one of the most popular vines for summer bloom.*

The nodding bell flowers of Clematis texensis 'Duchess of Albany' bloom from summer into fall.

Among the tallest clematis, Clematis montana *grows to 30 feet and is covered in spring with small fragrant flowers.*

Clematis 'Vyvyan Pennell' *blooms in spring and again in fall. Her spring flowers are double; her fall flowers are single.*

star performers, clematis is the favorite family of vines. Clematis, a large and varied group, are for the most part well-mannered, long-lived vines. If well planted and cared for, a clematis can live for 80 years or longer. Experts claim there are more than 300 species, and hybridizers have been at work since the 1850s. There is a clematis to please everyone, and I have yet to meet a variety I wouldn't recommend. Their's is a threaded passage as clematis gently wraps its petioles (leaf stems) around supports. Because the leaf stalks twist around their supports, clematis can't climb a flat surface without additional support. Clematis are most at home on the natural supports of trees and shrubs.

There are single-flowered clematis and double-flowered varieties with a generous overlap of petals. The best known of the doubles is 'Vyvyan Pennell', named after the wife of the breeder. When it first blooms in May and June on last year's growth, this vine is covered with large (6 to 7 inches across), double rosettes of violet-blue flowers, shaded with a blush of reddish purple in the middle of the 8 guard sepals. Climbing over 'Bonica', a pink shrub rose, it is a glorious sight. 'Vyvyan Pennell' is one of the few clematis I pick to add to bouquets or float in a bowl. The flowers last longer than a week in water, depending on how soon after bloom they are picked. Later, when 'Vyvyan Pennell' blooms in September, it will again be covered with flowers, only this time the flowers bloom on new growth and are single flowers, a lighter silver-violet in color.

While large-flowered clematis have an immediate impact, the small-flowered make up for their tiny size in the quantity of their blooms. The small-flowered varieties usually grow taller, and the profusion of flowers will delight you. It is also the species, rather than the large-flowered hybrids, that offer wonderful fragrance ranging from essence of vanilla, hot chocolate, almonds, lemons, primroses, cowslips and violets. *Clematis montana* has a honey scent, *C. montana* 'Wilsonii' smells like chocolate and *C. serralifolia* reminds one of lemons.

The seed pods of many clematis are pale balls of silvery or golden silk. These fine threads help the seeds to ride the wind to new areas of the garden where they plant themselves. (Some vines, such as sweet autumn clematis, are so prolific they become pests.) One, *C. vitalba*, when covered in seedpods, is nicknamed "old man's beard," "traveller's joy" and "snow in harvest."

The large-flowered varieties are divided into three classes: the spring-flowering clematis, that bloom during summer on last summer's growth (hardy to Zone 5); the patens, that bloom on old growth but earlier in the season (also hardy to Zone 5); and the Jackmanii, that bloom on new stems growing the same season (hardy to Zone 3). The Jackmanii have the longest bloom season, starting in summer and continuing until frost. In the coldest areas it is safest to lay the vines down and cover them for the winter. *Clematis maximowicziana*, a species from the Orient widely known as *C. paniculata*, the sweet autumn clematis, is a favorite of mine. The semievergreen vines grow to 30 feet, blooming in September and October with a profusion of 1-inch, white flowers deliciously scented (some say like hawthorn, others compare it to vanilla). The flowers are followed by silvery seed heads that self-seed and are wonderful for winter arrangements. The vine can be cut severely in late winter or after flowering and before the seeds form. A number of clematis have small, lantern-shaped flowers in summer and autumn. Included in this group are *C. orientalis* and *C. tangutica* varieties.

Cultural Information: Clematis grow best with sun at their tops and shade at their roots, the latter provided either by a groundcover or mulch. They are excellent vines for a north- or west-facing wall. If they are planted with a southern exposure or in a hot, dry location, they will need mulch and frequent watering. They should also have a shrub or taller perennial planted in front of them to protect their roots from the sun's direct rays. Fertile, well-drained soil with a high organic content (pH between 6 and 7) is best. Plant clematis at least 2 feet from any structure, especially cement footings that can suck moisture from surrounding soil. Bare-root plants purchased from catalogues are good travellers. To grow clematis up a tree or shrub, plant the vine under the outside circumference of the plant that is to support it. The vine will be able to grow into and over a shrub easily. To coax it up a tree, you'll need to train it up onto heavy string or wire to the lower branches, and from there it can find its own way. Water during periods of drought, and fertilize and replenish the soil yearly by mulching with 2 or 3 inches of compost, wood chips, pine needles or shredded leaves. Some gardeners recommend putting a flat, large (12-inch) stone near the base of a vine to make sure the soil stays cool and damp on the roots. Do not incorporate chemical fertilizer into the soil, as it may burn the roots. In colder climates where vines die back in winter, cut out any dead stems in early spring. Clematis take time to start their top growth as they must establish roots in their new home first. They won't reach their full potential for a few years.

The easiest way to propagate clematis is by layering (see page 32). It is more difficult to propagate by stem cuttings. To do so, take the cuttings in July. Unlike most plants, clematis stems root better between nodes (the joints) than at nodes.

The pruning of clematis is complicated by the various bloom times and heights of different varieties. The varieties that flower only on the current season's growth may benefit from yearly pruning, in order to keep the vine inbounds and where the flowers can be seen; all others can be left unpruned. For that matter, they can all be left unpruned, especially if they are to climb to some high point, as in a tree. As a healthy vine ages, it produces flowers on the highest part of the vine, leaving its long legs bare. Clematis can become a tangled mess, too. For those that need pruning, the question is, "when?" For pruning purposes, clematis are divided into three groups, A, B and C, each with

particular pruning instructions. Check the clematis chart (pages 48–49) for instructions on pruning different cultivars. These methods are recommended by expert Barry Fretwell, an English grower and hybridizer of clematis.

♦ *Group A.* The early spring-blooming varieties, which flower in May and June (*Clematis montana* is an example), bloom on the previous year's wood. They can be pruned after the last flower drops in early summer if they need to be cut back. Cut out the old wood that is without shoots, and then thin out weak shoots. When left unpruned to climb a tree, these clematis make incredible waterfalls of bloom, so do consider leaving plants in such situations unpruned.

♦ *Group B.* These clematis varieties flower continuously throughout summer on new growth, and should be pruned during the winter to the last pair of buds, about 12 inches above the ground; if they send shoots out from the ground, then prune almost to the ground. Spread the branches out horizontally as they grow, as this encourages more branching. This group includes all of the double-flowering types such as 'Vyvyan Pennell', which produces double flowers in spring on old wood, and single flowers in fall on new wood—a confusing habit. These clematis must not be pruned in fall, or you'll miss the double flowers. After they have first flowered in spring, the vine can be cleaned up without losing much of the fall

bloom. If the plants look good and you have the room, don't prune them. This group includes the varieties with the largest single flowers blooming in June and July on old wood, and with later bloom on new growth, with smaller flowers. If space allows they can be allowed to spread, and you will be rewarded with more blooms. To prune, pick your season of bloom. For large flowers in early summer, prune the plants after they have bloomed. For end-of-summer flowers, prune in spring.

♦ *Group C.* Clematis in this group need severe pruning. Most grow vigorously, from 10 to 20 feet in a season. These plants include large-flowered varieties such as *C. × jackmanii*, and the small-flowered varieties *C. orientalis* and *C. maximowicziana*. They can be pruned in February or March before new growth starts.

♦ *Group B/C.* Some clematis overlap these categories, and whether your vines are taking too much space can determine your pruning tactics. It may make sense to prune lightly one year and heavily another.

A common problem with clematis is wilt, generally thought to be caused by a fungus. Usually it doesn't kill the plant, but the stem should be cut back. Always plant a clematis with 2 to 3 inches of the stem buried. If you notice the stem dies back from wilt, do not remove the plant. Such plants frequently recover and send up new shoots from the buried stem. Clematis is rarely affected by other diseases or pests.

CLEMATIS CHARACTERISTICS

Name	Flower Description	Height	Bloom Time	Pruning Category
Clematis alpina 'Willy'	nodding, pale mauve pink, deep pink in center	8 to 12 feet	late spring, early summer	C
Clematis × durandii	single, 4- to 5-inch, intense indigo blue with yellow and white stamens	6 to 10 feet	summer	C
Clematis florida 'Alba Plena'	double, 3 inches across, greenish-white	6 to 10 feet	June to October	B
Clematis macropetala (downy clematis)	nodding open bells, 2 to 3 inches across, lavender-blue	8 to 12 feet	spring	A
Clematis maximowicziana (sweet autumn clematis)	single, 1 inch across, white	to 30 feet	fall	C
Clematis montana 'Rubens'	single, 2 to 2½ inches across, light pink	20 to 30 feet	May and June	A
Clematis tangutica	nodding 1- to 1½-inches-long, bell-shaped, buttercup yellow	10 to 15 feet	July to October	C
Clematis texensis 'Duchess of Albany'	bell-shaped, bright pink	8 to 12 feet	summer into fall	C
Clematis × jackmanii	single, 5 to 6 inches across, regal purple	12 to 30 feet	summer	B
'Dr. Ruppel'	single, 6- to 8-inch pinwheel, strawberry pink with deep carmine stripe	6 to 12 feet	early summer	B
'Duchess of Edinburgh'	double, 5 to 6 inches across, white	8 to 12 feet	May and June	B
'Elsa Spath'	single, 6 to 8 inches across, lavender-blue with reddish-purple stamens	8 to 10 feet	summer	B
'Ernest Markham'	single, 5 to 6 inches across, ruby red	12 to 15 feet	July to October	B/C
'General Sikorski'	single, 6 to 8 inches across, dark lavender with blend of red along the veins, cream stamens	8 to 12 feet	late spring and summer	B
'Hagley Hybrid'	single, 5 to 6 inches across, shell pink with purple anthers	6 to 8 feet	June to September	B/C
'Henryi'	single, 6 to 7 inches across, pure white	6 to 10 feet	June and September	B
'H. F. Young'	single, 6 to 8 inches, bright blue	8 feet	May and June, again in September	B
'Lincoln Star'	single, raspberry-pink with lavender edges and dark stamens	4 to 5 feet	May and June, again in August	B
'Madame Edouard Andre'	single, 5 inches across, wine red with creamy stamen	6 to 8 feet	July to September	C
'Marie Boisselot'	single, 6 to 8 inches across, pale pink fading to white with yellow stamen	6 to 12 feet	summer	B
'Nelly Moser'	single, 5 to 7 inches across, pinwheel of pink striped with deep carmine	8 to 12 feet	early summer, again early fall	B

'Niobe'	single, 5 to 6 inches across, dark ruby red, yellow stamens	8 to 10 feet	early summer to fall	B/C
'Ramona'	single, 6 to 8 inches across, lavender-blue	10 to 20 feet	late spring, summer	Best left unpruned
'Star of India'	single, 5 to 6 inches across, plum-red background, red pinwheel stripe	up to 20 feet	all summer	C
'Ville de Lyon'	single, 5 to 6 inches across, carmine with deep crimson edges and golden stamens	10 to 12 feet	midsummer to fall	B/C
'Vyvyan Pennell'	double in spring, single in fall, 6 to 7 inches across, violet	6 to 8 feet	May and June, again in September	B

Unless noted all flower descriptions are for flat, many-petalled flowers.

Clerodendrum (cler-oh-DEN-drum) ***Clerodendrum Thomsoniae*, bleeding heart vine, glory bower,** TP, E, ◐
Zone: 10
Height: 10 to 15 feet
Colors: Scarlet and white
Characteristics: Upwardly mobile, bleeding heart vine is not a sprawler, but twines as it grows up. It is from West Africa and blooms freely from summer to fall. The broad, hairy and deeply veined, 3- to 6-inch leaves contrast with the tiny, deep scarlet flowers that resemble bleeding hearts. Each flower is surrounded by white ornamental bracts, as if it were presenting its heart gift wrapped. The flowers hang in clusters in order to make their presence known. When grown in hanging baskets or tubs in the North, bleeding heart vine will stay small and can be moved indoors easily before frost. It will flower even when small in a 6-inch pot. In tropical climates it can be planted directly in the ground. Even if the top is killed by cold, the vine will not suffer much as it blooms on new wood the next season.
Cultural Information: A tropical, vinelike shrub, bleeding heart vine is accustomed to 60° F. nights and 70° F. days. It can be grown easily on a windowsill with bright, indirect or filtered light. A chill sends it into hibernation. Plant it in a packaged potting soil and water frequently to keep the soil evenly moist, but not soggy. Fertilize container-grown vines every other week with a half-strength solution during the growing and blooming season. Pinch back the young stems to encourage branching, and provide strong supports for the vine to twine on. Due to the weight of the plant, it will need to be tied up as it grows. Remove spent flowers and dead twigs in summer to encourage reblooming. Prune after the vine finishes flowering in winter. White flies can be a problem.

Climbing fig; see ***Ficus***

Climbing hydrangea; see ***Hydrangea***

Climbing roses; see ***Rosa***

Climbing snapdragon; see ***Asarina***

Clockvine; see ***Thunbergia***

Cobaea (ko-BEE-a) ***Cobaea scandens*, cup-and-saucer vine, cathedral bells,** TP, A, F, ○
Zones: 9 to 10
Height: 15 to 25 feet in one season; 40 feet as a perennial
Colors: Purple, white
Characteristics: Cup-and-saucer vine is named for the shape of its flowers, which indeed resemble teacups (like the Mad Hatter's, perhaps?) as they hang upside-down on the vine. Some cups grow to 2½ inches deep. The flowers of the common variety open pale green and gradually turn lilac, then purple with white pinstripes. A white variety ('Alba') is also available. The individual

Clerodendrum thomsoniae presents each flower surrounded by a white ornamental bract, as if presenting its heart gift wrapped.

Cup-and-saucer vine is named for the shape of its flowers, which resemble teacups hanging upside-down on the vine.

Both the velvety purple beans and the purple or white, sweet pea–like flowers of Dolichos lablab *are decorative.*

blooms make long-lasting cut flowers. In bud the flowers have an unpleasant fragrance, but are honey-scented when mature. The green leaves are veined with purple. The stems climb easily without much help, using foot-long corkscrew tendrils hooked at the end; they climb almost any surface without support. This is a good vine for growing in a greenhouse. In mild climates it lives outdoors from year to year, eventually reaching 40 feet or more and blooming heavily from spring to fall.

Cultural Information: Start seed early indoors (germination may take 14 days or more). If sown outdoors in cool, wet weather, the hard-coated seeds may rot. The vines take approximately 4 months to flower and should be started indoors in February or March in northern areas. In southern gardens, sow directly outdoors in spring. Stick the flat seeds vertically on their edge in soil rather than laying them flat. This will prevent them from rotting in wet soil. They should barely be covered, and kept moist but not wet. Growth is rapid in warm weather, and the vines will continue to grow after light frost.

Common hop; see *Humulus*

Confederate star jasmine; see *Trachelospermum*

Coral honeysuckle; see *Lonicera*

Costa Rican nightshade; see *Solanum*

Cow itch; see *Campsis*

Creeping fig; see *Ficus*

Creeping glorinia; see *Asarina*

Crimson starglory; see *Mina*

Cup-and-saucer vine; see *Cobaea*

Dipladenia; see *Mandevilla*

Dolichos (DOL-ik-os) *Dolichos lablab,* **hyacinth bean,** TP, A ○
Zones: 9 and 10
Height: 10 or more feet
Colors: Purple, white
Characteristics: Hyacinth bean's leaves appear from a distance to have a maroon tint, especially on the underside. Upon a closer look it is obvious that it is the showy, deep maroon veins running through the leaves that give the foliage its wonderful color. Later, when the purple or white sweet-pea-like flowers appear (singly or in clusters), followed by flat, velvety purple "beans" 2 to 2½ inches long, the vine is even more striking. A tropical vine, perennial in its native climate, hyacinth bean grows quickly and densely. The broad, oval, light green leaves are divided fanlike into 3 leaflets, 3 to 6 inches long. Here in North America it is grown as an ornamental, occasionally eaten in salads; it is grown for food in the tropics.
Cultural Information: Hyacinth bean likes moderately fertile soil kept reasonably moist. It does not transplant well and is

best sown directly where it is to grow. Grown from seed it takes approximately 14 days to germinate when temperatures are 70° to 80° F. It will bloom from seed in approximately 3 months. It is perennial in Zones 9 and 10. It climbs by twining, and needs a support to grow on.

Dutchman's pipe; see *Aristolochia*

Eccremocarpus (ek-rem-o-KARP-us) *Eccremocarpus scaber,* **Chilean glory vine,** TP, A ○
Zones: 9 to 10
Height: 8 to 12 feet
Colors: Orange, red, pink, yellow, bicolors
Characteristics: Clusters of orange-scarlet, narrow, lopsidedly bottle-shaped, 1¼-inch-long flowers dangle from the lacy foliage of Chilean glory vine the whole summer long. The delicate foliage is made up of many small leaflets. The vine is self-clinging as its tendrils twine around supports. It has a semi-

Eccremacarpus scaber, the Chilean glory vine, is grown as an annual for its summer flowers.

shrubby growth, growing wide as it climbs. Chilean glory vine is a South American native from Chile and Peru. In mild areas it is perennial, returning even if cut down by frost. It will usually grow back up from the roots. _Eccremocarpus s. aurantiacus_ has warm, amber yellow flowers, and _E. s. coccineus_ has coppery crimson flowers with darker foliage. _E. s. roseus_ has pinkish flowers.

Cultural Information: Chilean glory vine is an easily grown annual, blooming from seed the first year in northern zones and living for years in frost-free areas. It can be direct sown where it is to grow, as it flowers early. For earlier bloom, it can be started indoors in March to transplant outdoors after all danger of frost is past. Plant in well-drained, loamy soil.

English ivy; see _**Hedera**_

**Euonymus**   (yew-ON-im-us)
**Euonymus fortunei,** **wintercreeper,** P, E ◑ ○ ●
Zones: 5 to 10
Height: 20 feet
Color: —
Characteristics: Wintercreeper is an evergreen vine that forms a spreading, closely woven mat even in northern climates. It is most often used as a groundcover. It has tiny rootlets along its stem that cling to rocks, trees and walls as it climbs. Most commonly grown varieties produce inconspicuous flowers and virtually hidden berries (birds have a way of finding the berries). Some varieties are variegated with yellow, silver-white or even pink splotches in the leaves. The baby win-

Wintercreeper (Euonymus fortunei) _creeps along the ground or up a wall or tree._

Yellow-leaved euonymus bring a little sunshine into any shady area.

tercreeper 'Minima' has tiny ½-inch-long leaves, green with yellow centers. It always looks neat and well groomed, and is useful as a woodland groundcover, perfect for underplanting with miniature daffodils, checkered lilies or shooting stars. 'Carrierei' is a shrubby variety. 'Gracilis' has variegated foliage with white or cream that takes on a pink tint in cold weather. 'Sunspot' and 'Variegata' are yellow-leaved types. In hot sun, wintercreeper performs better than ivy. Surprisingly, it is also a dependable broad-leaved evergreen where temperatures dip below 0° F. At times it might turn brown and die back, but will usually return.

Cultural Information: Wintercreepers perform best in partial shade in moist, well-drained soil. Their roots are shallow and easily adapt to being planted in rock walls or rock gardens. Pruning is rarely necessary as wintercreepers are slow creepers. They are easily propagated by stem cuttings in spring. They can be susceptible to scale; this is controlled by dormant oil sprayed in early summer.

Evening trumpet flower; see *Gelsenium*

Everlasting pea; see *Lathyrus*

Ficus (FIK-us) ***Ficus pumila*, creeping fig, climbing fig,** TP, E, ○ ◑
Zones: 9 to 10
Height: Almost no limit if given enough time
Color: Grown for its green foliage

Characteristics: The tiny heart-shaped leaves on creeping figs grow on crisscrossing stems. Flattening itself against any surface, this vine grows by attaching itself with the tenacity of barnacles to wood, masonry, even metal, as it climbs and forms a dense mat. It can completely cover a three- or four-story building, windows and all, if left unpruned. Its small-leaved, self-clinging habit make it a popular vine for topiaries large and small. At Disney World and the New York Botanical Garden, 4-foot-high topiary frames are planted with plugs of creeping fig that fill out and cover them in 3 months for display in the gardens. This is a popular climber for greenhouse walls and hanging baskets. Like ivy, it withstands shade, supports itself with aerial roots and changes its characteristics when it reaches the top of its support, developing larger leaves, a bushier habit, flowers and inedible figs. It is slow growing in its youth, but increases in vigor as it ages. It is native to China, Japan and Australia.
Cultural Information: Not particularly fussy as long as the soil is well drained, creeping fig is easy to grow. However, if it is being grown as a topiary, it is important to mist it daily. It won't grow in the sun on a hot, south-facing wall; it makes an attempt, but languishes and turns yellow.

Ficus pumila is a tender perennial that flattens itself against any surface, clinging as it grows, which is why it is popular for covering topiaries large and small.

Five-leaf akebia; see *Akebia*

Fleece vine; see *Polygonum*

Gelsemium (je-SEEM-ium) ***Gelsemium sempervirens*, Carolina jasmine, evening trumpet flower,** P, F, E, ○ ◑
Zones: 7 to 10
Height: 20 feet
Color: Yellow
Characteristics: A native of the southern United States and Mexico, Carolina jasmine is a climbing shrub and the state flower of South Carolina. Its fragrance is similar to that of

Carolina jasmine (Gelsemium sempervirens) is a climbing shrub and the state flower of South Carolina.

true jasmine. The yellow trumpet-shaped flowers are 1 to 1½ inches long and bloom in clusters from late winter through spring. Although "sempervirens" in Latin means evergreen, Carolina jasmine has semi-evergreen foliage in northern areas where the foliage color turns rusty during the cold months. This vine is more of a leaner than a twister, even though the reddish stems will twist halfheartedly around supports. It must be tied to a support; if grown on a trellis or arbor, it will cascade down to swing in the breeze. It can be grown as a groundcover if kept trimmed back to 3 feet. It is easily grown indoors in a hanging basket, where it will trail over the sides. It is not usually hardy in areas where the temperature dips to 15° F., but in a well-sheltered site, it can survive to Zone 6. *Gelsemium sempervirens* 'Plena' is the double-flowering form. All parts of the vine are poisonous, which perhaps explains why insects leave it alone.

Cultural Information: In the South, Carolina jasmine is a rampant evergreen that has naturalized along roadsides and woodlands. It adapts to different conditions, but it prefers soil rich in compost or dehydrated manure. Compost and/or manure should be added yearly as a mulch, allowing nutrients to be carried to the vine's roots with the rain water. This will also help keep the roots cool and the soil moist. A moist but well-drained soil is best, although it can survive periods of drought.

Carolina jasmine needs

nights of 50° F. or colder to set its golden buds. This can be a problem if the vine is growing indoors. Otherwise, it is fairly easy-going on a sunny windowsill if fertilized monthly, and if the soil is kept moist during the active growing period. In late fall and early winter the soil can be allowed to dry out between waterings. Prune only after the flowers bloom in spring, not in late fall or winter, when you might be cutting off next year's flowers. Carolina jasmine can be grown from seed or from stem cuttings taken in spring.

German ivy; see ***Senecio***

Giant granadilla; see ***Passiflora***

Glory bower; see ***Clerodendrum***

Golden clematis; see ***Clematis***

Golden trumpet vine; see ***Allamanda***

Goldflame honeysuckle; see ***Lonicera***

Gold-net honeysuckle; see ***Lonicera***

Grape ivy; see ***Cissus***

Hall's honeysuckle; see ***Lonicera***

Hedera (HED-er-a) ***Hedera canariensis,*** **Algerian ivy;** ***Hedera helix,*** **English ivy;** P, D, ○ ◑ ●
Zones: 4 to 10
Height: 40 or more feet

Hedera helix *is available in more than 60 varieties, including 'Goldheart'.*

Hedera helix, *the English ivy, holds its leaves throughout the winter.*

Color: Green foliage
Characteristics: With its dark green, leathery leaves and its dependable, uniform and neat habits English ivy is the most popular ivy for shady areas. It roots as it grows, knitting the soil together, and when grown on banks it helps to prevent erosion. Ivies have small aerial roots that cling tenaciously to whatever they touch, making them easy to train into topiaries, to climb walls or to drape

over containers. Although a slow grower, *Hedera* is long lived. A specimen more than 400 years old has been reported growing in Ginac, France.

Ivies, the garden's work-horses, are hard to beat for enhancing the beauty of other flowering plants whether grown on a wall with a climbing rose or with another flowering vine on top, draped from a container, or sprawling along the ground to edge a path.

The colonists brought many fancy-leaved varieties of ivy from England. English ivies (*Hedera helix*) alone are available in more than 60 varieties, with lobed, fan-shaped, diamond-shaped, bird's-foot, round or heart-shaped leaves, and smooth, ruffled, wavy or curled surfaces and edges, with foliage that ranges in size from a dime to a dinner plate. Ivies grow in every shade of green, some touched with gray, others with yellow or even purple. Every possible style of variegation (streaked, splashed, spotted, speckled, edged, marbled and veined) is to be found in this family. There are almost infinite varieties from which to choose. The large-leaved (5 to 7 inches across) variegated Algerian ivy (*Hedera canariensis* 'Variegata') with its gray-green leaves edged with blotches of white boasts distinctive wine-red twigs and stems. *H. canariensis* isn't as hardy as many of the other ivies (just to Zone 6), but it is widely grown as a groundcover in California. New roots form along the stem as it grows. *H. helix* 'Buttercup' is a golden variety, 'Glacier' has

snow white variegation, and 'Goldenheart', one of the most popular, has a gold splash in the center of its leaves. The yellow and gold varieties need more light than the plain green ivies.

Ivies, easily grown indoors, are beneficial to our health. NASA research shows *Hedera helix* destroys benzene, a carcinogen found in cigarette smoke, paints and solvents. The small-leafed ivies are popular as houseplants, in offices, for hanging baskets and to cover small indoor topiaries. Even when planted alone in a container, they bring a bit of green color and life to dim, poorly lighted areas.

As ivy matures it forms stiff stems, which bear clusters of small greenish flowers followed by black berries. The berries stay through the winter and are loved by birds. Their seed, however, can be mildly toxic to humans. Once established, ivy can be cut off at the ground and ripped from the structure it covers if the structure needs repair or repainting; the ivy will quickly reestablish itself over the next few years. Ivy will not damage mortar or bricks. However, if mortar is loose, ivy could aggravate the situation as it grows. If you long for ivy-covered brick, first check the mortar between the bricks, scraping it with a knife. If it crumbles, the structure should be remortared before ivy is planted, or the ivy will loosen it where it is crumbling. (In the case of some old, crumbling walls, the ivy actually holds the wall together.) Ivy should not be allowed to grow onto a roof

as it can push between shingles, leaving an opening. It will not harm tree trunks. However, if the ivy becomes too dense at the top of a tree and shuts out light, it could kill the tree. On a small tree ivy may become so heavy it deforms the tree's branches as it grows.

Cultural Information: Ivies tolerate extreme conditions, from full sun to shade, wet to dry, and even polluted air. They also adapt to most soils. Algerian ivy is best grown in part shade, to protect it from winter burn in colder areas. In hot, southern climates vines are better planted in part shade. While not fussy about soil conditions, vines find a well-drained, compost-enriched soil ideal. If they are to grow up a wall, plant them a foot from the wall and space the plants 12 to 18 inches apart. A mulch at their feet will hold the moisture and keep weeds from sprouting until the vines are established, at which point weeds won't have a chance. Ivies are propagated easily from cuttings started in moist sand or water and can be grown as minimum-care houseplants.

Heart-seed; see ***Cardiospermom***

Honeysuckle; see ***Lonicera***

Hop; see ***Humulus***

Hummingbird vine; see ***Asarina***

Humulus (HEW-mew-lus) ***Humulus lupulus*, common hops; *Humulus scandens*; *Humulus japonicus*, Japanese hop;** P, A, D, ○ ◑

Zones: 3 to 10

Height: Annual hops, 10 to 20 feet; perennial hops, 35 or more feet

Color: Green

Characteristics: Hops are to be found as both annual and perennial varieties that die back to the ground in fall. The Japanese, or annual, hop (*Humulus japonicus*) is often grown as a quick and temporary solution to cover unsightly areas or buildings. It grows 10, 20 or more feet in a single season, and is able to withstand wind. Its 6- to 8-inch-wide, bright green leaves provide dense cover. Male and female flowers are produced on different plants. The female plants produce green, pineconelike flowers. Japanese hop can become a pest as it self-seeds readily.

Humulus lupulus, common or perennial hop, is a European and Asian native that has become naturalized in the United States. This hop is grown for the fruit used in making beer; it is not often grown as an ornamental. The vines climb by twining as they grow. They will need the strong support of an arch, pillar, porch or arbor trellis. This vine makes an excellent screen. 'Aureus' (hardy to Zone 3) is the golden hop that lights up shady places.

Cultural Information: Ordinary, well-drained soil is all that is required for these easy-to-grow vines. Quicker growth will result from compost-rich soil, although the vines are good at withstanding drought. Japanese hops can be directly planted outdoors after all danger of frost, and often reseed the following spring. The common hop should be cut to the ground yearly, after frost turns it brown, and will quickly grow back to the same size the following spring. Perennial varieties can be propagated in spring by root division or cuttings of young shoots, 3 or 4 inches long. The thick part of the roots are planted up, just below soil level.

Hyacinth bean; see ***Dolichos***

Hydrangea (hy-DRAN-jee-a) ***Hydrangea anomala petiolaris*, climbing hydrangea,** P, D, ○ ◑

Zones: 5 to 10

Height: 75 or more feet

Color: White

The golden hops gives the effect of sunlight even on overcast days.

Climbing hydrangea climbs up and over a building at Bayberry Nursery on Long Island. Its spring flowers bloom with abandon.

Characteristics: Native to Japan and China, climbing hydrangea arrived here in the 1860s. For several weeks in June, the climbing hydrangea is an eye-catcher covered with fluffy white flower clusters, each 6 to 8 inches across. Individual flowers within the clusters are normally 1¼ inches across. This is one of the best and most versatile of the woody clinging vines. It doesn't need help climbing because it clings, by sending out aerial rootlets—or fastholds—that can grab onto brick, stone or wood. While it climbs the wall, pressing its stems flat, it can also support lateral branches 3 feet away from the wall. The leaves are finely toothed, oval and shiny; they turn a golden autumn color with the frost. Slow to start when first transplanted, it sits for a few years while establishing roots before sudden acceleration helps it easily cover an unattractive area. Climbing hydrangea is beautiful scaling the trunk of a large tree or covering a wall. The vine is deciduous, but even when baring its winter skeleton of rigid, reddish-brown stems, it is ornamental.

Cultural Information: Climbing hydrangea prefers a rich organic, slightly acid soil. It grows in sun or shade but needs to be kept moist for the early years until it is established; then it will tolerate drought. Prune the vine to maintain shape and size. It

Moonflowers open at day's end, fragrant and often 6 inches across.

'Heavenly Blue' morning glories open in the morning but close as evening approaches.

doesn't harm the surface on which it climbs. Hydrangea can be propagated from stem cuttings or grown from seed.

Ipomoea (eye-po-MEE-a)
Ipomoea alba, **moonflower;** *Ipomea batatas* **'Blackie', black morning glory, black-vined sweet potato;** *Ipomoea purpurea,* **morning glory;** A, F, ○

Height: Moonflower, 15 to 30 feet; 'Blackie', 3 to 6 feet; morning glory, 6 inches to 15 feet

Colors: Blue, white, pink, bicolors

Characteristics: The *Ipomoea* family is full of wonderful, ornamental climbing vines. Moonflowers light up the garden at night and on cloudy days. They are vigorous climbers with large, full, round, intensely fragrant, purest-white flowers. The flowers are often banded green, 5 to 6 inches across and 4 inches deep. They open early in the evening and close before noon the following day; however, if the day is overcast and dark, they are fooled into staying open later. Their heart-shaped leaves are large, reaching up to 8 inches. Even without the flowers, the large leaves are attractive. In frost-free climates, moonflowers are perennial. The stems can be prickly, as they are covered with fine hairs, so be careful when handling the vine. They are also quick twining and stems can complete a circle around a support in 3 hours. Buds can be cut and used in an evening flower arrangement, but will be gone by morning.

Moonflower's sweet, heavenly scent is concentrated in the oil between the central bands inside the open flower. The perfumed oil attracts night-flying moths, which fertilize the flowers. Each flower lasts one night, but the buds come fast and furious till frost.

The morning glory, with heart-shaped leaves and sunny circles of bright color, is a versatile and beautiful annual. Morning glories can camouflage unsightly buildings or trash bins, or be trained to grow over hedges, other climbers or large bushes to make then appear to be flowering. They can be planted at the base of sunflowers, after the sunflowers have been growing a few weeks, when they can support the weight of the vine. Morning glories are popular growing up drainpipes and mailboxes. They will not damage their "host."

Morning glories have tendrils that reach out and twine around whatever is in their path to pull themselves up. They easily grow down from large pots or window boxes, or scrambling along the ground they help to brighten hillsides or barren land. In tropical areas of the United States and the Caribbean Islands, morning glories, although still beautiful, are invasive, covering plants along the roadside, climbing trees and anything else in their path. They reseed with abandon, as if working on a massive repopulation scheme. Each flower lasts only a day, but there seem always to be more flowers waiting in the wings to open. The "waiting flowers" are pointed buds with petals that overlap in a spiral at the tip, and they are decorative in their own right. As the sun gets hotter, or as evening approaches, they finish their short bloom by pursing their lips and sucking them in, leaving their funny faces to hang on the vine for another day or two.

'Heavenly blue', with 4- to 5-inch sky blue flowers is one of the tallest, and 'Early Call', with mixed colors, is one of the shortest. 'Scarlet O'Hara', an AAS winner with crimson-carmine flowers, and 'Pearly Gates', an AAS winner with enormous, 4½-inch, shining white flowers, are also tall growers. There are dwarf cultivars for hanging baskets and pots; 'Roman Candy' has rose-colored flowers, and white picoteed edges on its silver-dusted leaves. All varieties are adaptable to an 8-inch pot, but they look better when grown several to a 12-inch pot, or combined with other annuals in larger pots. Morning glories are easily grown from seed and are adaptable to the smallest spaces. *I. batatas* 'Blackie' has lacquered black stems and lustrous foliage so purple it looks black. The leaves, deeply lobed, make a sharp contrast when combined in containers with green-leafed plants. The stems grow to 3 feet long. It is grown like a morning glory but doesn't flower. All parts of the vines are poisonous.

Cultural Information: Seed of morning glories and moonflowers have a hard shell that makes it difficult for the plant embryo to break through. To speed germination, soak seed in water at room temperature several hours before planting, to soften the outer shell, or score the outer shell with a file to allow the embryo to break through. Better yet, do both. A higher percentage of germination will result. The seeds can be planted outdoors early in spring, but they won't grow until the soil and air temperature are constantly warm. The vines need protection from strong winds and a trellis, string or a fence to wind around as they pull themselves up. They prefer poor, well-drained soil, and will flower more if the soil is left unfertilized. They can be direct sown after the soil warms. Seeds sit and wait to be warmed, sometimes rotting if the soil is too wet and too cold. They can be started indoors 6 to 8 weeks before they are planted outdoors. When outdoor temperatures are between 65° and 70° F., the seeds will germinate quickly, usually between 7 and 21 days. Morning glories bloom in 65 to 70 days, and moonflowers bloom later, approximately 90 to 100 days after sowing. 'Blackie', grown for its leaves, won't bloom over the summer.

Ipomea versicolor; see *Mina lobata*

Japanese creeper; see *Parthenocissus tricuspidata*

Japanese hop; see *Humulus*

Japanese ivy; see *Parthenocissus tricuspidata*

Japanese wisteria; see *Wisteria*

Jasmine; see *Jasminum*

Jasmine nightshade; see *Solanum*

Jasminum (JAS-min-um) *Jasminum nucliflorum,* jasmine; *Jasminum officinale grandiflorum,* common jasmine; *Jasminum polyanthum,* winter jasmine; *Jasminum sambac* **'Maid of Orleans',** Arabian tea jasmine; *Jasminum* **species,** (formerly *Jasminum odoratissimum*); *Jasminum nitidum,* royal jasmine, shining jasmine; TP, F, E, ○ ◑
Zones: 9 and 10
Height: 10 to 20 feet
Color: White
Characteristics: Jasmine is one of the most celebrated of flower fragrances. It is an essential ingredient in a number of expen-

The fragrant pinwheel-shaped flowers of Jasmine nitidum *bloom almost continuously.*

Jasmine polyanthum's *rosy pink buds bloom in winter, starting around Valentine's day, with masses of deliciously sweet-scented, starry white flowers.*

sive perfumes (Joy, for example) and used extensively in the Orient for flavoring tea and scenting religious observances. There are more than 200 species of jasmine. Figuring out which vines are real jasmine can be confusing, as many are similar in fragrance and flower, have the common name of jasmine, and in many cases the species name *jasminoides*. There is the Confederate jasmine (*Trachelospermum jasminoides*), the Cape jasmine (*Gardenia jasminoides* 'Prostrata') and the Carolina jasmine (*Gelsemium sempervirens*), to name a few. Even the common names of true jasmine are confusing. Both *J. nudiflorum* and *J. polyanthum* are winter jasmine, *J. nitidum* and *J. officinale grandiflorum* are angel-wing jasmine, and *J. nitidum* and *J. polyanthum* are star jasmine. So if you're not sure which vine you're growing, you're in good company. Just remind yourself jasmine are simply meant to be enjoyed.

Jasminum polyanthum blooms in winter, starting around Valentine's Day, with masses of deliciously sweet-scented, starry white flowers that open from rosy pink buds. Tovah Martin, an expert on jasmines and a well-known garden writer, says its scent is "tainted by a touch of fermented citrus." I find it irresistible. The fragrance can be overpowering in a small area, but is wonderful outdoors. The individual flowers are small, 1 inch across, but they bloom in large clusters. The jasmines take pride in their personal appearance, and the flowers fall from the vine before they discolor; the vines always look good. I gather the still-fresh and fragrant fallen blooms and use them for table decorations. It can be used as a cut flower, too. *J. polyanthum* is hardy to 20° F. and prefers bright, but not direct, sun. It needs cool temperatures and more water when it blooms. A cool, barely heated sunroom or enclosed, unheated porch will work for northern gardeners.

Often pruned as shrubs in southern gardens, winter-blooming jasmine make good greenhouse and houseplants for northern gardeners. They can be moved outdoors for the summer until fall, when a month of cold nights (to 45° F.) will set the buds. In southern climates they can live outdoors. If killed back by cold, it usually recovers. It can withstand 20° F. if chilled gradually. If grown touching a cold window, the stems will brown.

Jasminum nitidum is often called the royal jasmine and the shining jasmine, a name suggested by the polished look of its glossy leaves. The pinwheel-shaped flowers, 2 inches across are made up of from 9 to 11 petals, and bloom almost continuously, mostly in groups of threes, at times four or five. They have a pink tint when in bud, and a few pink streaks on the back of the petals when in flower. The shining jasmine requires a long, warm growing period to bloom. When young, it is not reliable where temperatures go below 25° F.; later it can tolerate colder weather. In the early years, protect any outdoor plants if frost is expected. Given conditions it likes, it can reach a height of 20 feet. It makes a good container plant or a shrubby groundcover, blooming almost year 'round.

Jasminum officinale grandiflorum, the common jasmine, has a potent evening scent and is hardy to Zone 7 if planted in a protected location. This is the jasmine famed as an ingredient in French perfume. *J. nudiflorum* is the short-changed family member; it is without fragrance. It has yellow flowers and blooms in winter with protection as far north as Zone 6. Hybrids of *J. sambac* are the most popular for growing as houseplants as they prefer temperatures of 60° F. and above. 'Maid of Orleans' has semidouble flowers that bloom off and on throughout the year. The flowers open white and age to wine-red before falling.

Cultural Information: Jasmine takes a wide variety of soils—even sandy—but are not tolerant of salt air. If they are planted in too windy an area or without half a day of sun or bright light, they refuse to bloom. Any nonflowering branches should be pruned out. Jasmine can be pruned after flowering to shape them. The soil should not be too dry, so water regularly. Go easy with the fertilizer, as too much can cause leaf burn and result in fewer flowers. Propagate jasmine with cuttings from the current year's growth in fall, or by layering in summer.

Kolomikta vine; see ***Actinidia***

Kudzu vine; see ***Pueraria***

Lathyrus (LATH-i-rus) *Lathyrus latifolius,* everlasting pea; *Lathyrus odoratus,* sweet pea; A and P, CF, F (annual, not perennial), D, ○ ◑
Zones: L. latifolius, 4 to 10
Height: Dwarf varieties, 9 to 15 inches; tall annual varieties, 5 to 6 feet; perennial varieties, 9 feet
Colors: All colors except yellow; bicolors, mottled, striped
Characteristics: The airy blossoms of sweet pea, shaped like miniature sun bonnets, can be single colors, bicolors, mottled or striped. The colors themselves vary from pale, soft tints to deep tones. The flowers on the perennial and annual sweet pea are similar; the important difference is that only the annual sweet peas are fragrant. At the turn of the century, the annual sweet pea was Burpee's best-selling flower, and as such it graced many a catalog cover. Flowers with a longer bloom season and greater adaptability have since surpassed it in popularity, but it deserves to be grown for its sweet fragrance and the beauty of its graceful, curving vines covered with delicate, old-fashioned flowers. Plant sweet peas where they can climb on a fence, trellis or netting, or on supports up the side of a building. The bush types are good for edging, and in borders and window boxes. Not only beautiful, sweet peas have had their impact on science, too. These are the plants with which Gregor Mendel did his early experiments when founding the science of genetics.

Annual varieties include

The annual sweet pea (Lathyrus odoratus) *was the most popular garden flower at the turn of the century.*

Burpee's dwarf 'Patio' and 'Bijou', bushy plants that don't need staking. 'Patio' has larger flowers, but 'Bijou' blooms earlier and longer. Tall, vining annual varieties are 'Early Multiflora Gigantea', an early blooming, heat-resistant variety, and Burpee's 'Galaxy', a multiflowered climber with bloom from early summer on; many of 'Galaxy's stems have five or more large flowers. 'Old Spice' is a very fragrant mix with many bicolors and striped flowers. Sweet peas are long-lasting cut flowers. The 12-inch stems of the tall varieties make them easy to pick. The perennial sweet pea blooms in clusters of 1½-inch, white, rose and magenta flowers. The vine, covered with flowers in July, has scattered blooms all the rest of summer. Although it can be invasive, it is a good vine for holding a bank.

Cultural Information: Annual sweet peas like well-drained, neutral to lime soil, rich in humus. Plant outdoors in spring as early as the soil can be prepared. Sweet peas do best where weather is cool. For my Zone 7 garden, I start them indoors the first week of January and then move the plants outdoors on St. Patrick's Day. I find if they are well established with deep roots going into the hot weather of summer, they will bloom longer and better, often all summer long.

Soak the seed in lukewarm water overnight or for 24 hours to soften the seed coat and speed germination. It is best to sprinkle Legume Aid or Burpee Booster on the soil in the spot you are planting; these organic preparations put millions of live nitrogen-fixing bacteria into the soil, enabling the roots to make use of atmospheric nitrogen. This will improve growth and increase the number of flowers. Mulch to keep roots cool, and water deeply and regularly. For earliest, best and longest bloom in northern areas where spring quickly turns into hot summer, we recommend starting seed indoors (in peat pots) as early as January. After heavy frost, but while weather is still cool, move the plants outdoors to a well-drained, sunny area. Space the plants 6 inches apart, depending on variety. The seeds will germinate in 14 to 20 days if the temperature is kept near 55° F. The flowers will bloom in approximately 80 to 90 days, depending on the variety. The perennial sweet pea is easily grown from seed to bloom the following year, and it may also be purchased as potted plants.

In the South and Southwest, sweet peas are planted from fall to winter. Sweet peas are ideally suited for spring growth in the coastal regions of the Northwest and New England, and they do nicely in a cool greenhouse. Cut regularly for indoor bouquets and to help extend the bloom season. All parts of this plant are poisonous.

Lonicera (lon-ISS-er-a) ***Lonicera japonica halliana,*** **honeysuckle;** ***Lonicera × heckrottii* 'Goldflame',** **coral honeysuckle;** ***Lonicera × brownii* Dropmore Scarlet';** ***Lonicera periclymenum* 'Serotina Florida';** ***Lonicera japonica* 'Aureo-reticulata',** **gold-net honeysuckle;** P, F, E (in southern zones), D (in northern zones), ○ ◑
Zones: 5 to 9
Height: 15 to 30 feet
Colors: Yellow, coral, red, white
Characteristics: The most commonly seen honeysuckle is the Japanese honeysuckle vine, which tosses long sprays of slender, tubular flowers into the air. The flowers sit on the stems in pairs and, upon opening at evening, are pure white and especially fragrant, attracting night-flying moths. After fertilization, the corollas turn pale yellow. Honeysuckle needs wire netting or a lattice to twine about, but otherwise is not fussy. It thrives even at the seashore and blooms, off and

Lonicera japonica halliana, *the most commonly grown honeysuckle, can be a rampant grower that crowds out other plants.*

Lonicera japonica 'Aureo-reticulata' *is a well-behaved, short Japanese honeysuckle grown for its golden foliage.*

on, all summer. In full bloom in June, Japanese honeysuckle has sporadic bloom for the rest of the summer; I have even found blooms in December that have survived light frost. The common yellow and white, very fragrant honeysuckle, *L. japonica halliana* (Hall's honeysuckle), runs rampant when given perfect conditions, especially in the South where it takes to the road. There the growth of this plant is a free-for-all that isn't stopped by freezing winters. The vine travels at high speed, spreading by runners and seeds. Birds help to spread the seeds, as they love the black berries. It covers thousands of acres in the South, a tangle of vines covering trees and shrubs, crowding out native plants. It is a better be-

haved vine in gardens north of Pennsylvania. When we purchased our house, these plants formed an arbor over the front door where they had been planted more than 80 years ago. Everyone who enters our home during the course of the summer passes first through a fragrant tunnel.

Other better-behaved varieties include *L. × heckrottii* 'Goldflame', which grows to approximately 15 feet. It is coral in bud, opening to deep pink or reddish purple flowers with yellow throats. The flowers are showier than those of Japanese honeysuckle, though they lack its wonderful fragrance; they bloom through the summer and attract hummingbirds. 'Dropmore Scarlet' (*L. × brownii*) is a red form (not fragrant) that grows in Zones 3 to 9. *L. periclymenum* 'Serotina Florida' has fragrant flowers best described as narrow, flaring trumpets arranged as spokes of a wheel. Each trumpet is crimson, but together they flare open to a seemingly random mix that includes creamy white, yellow and dark red. Blooming from early summer to frost, this is a more compact vine than the common honeysuckle, growing to 20 feet, even in partial shade in Zones 5 to 9. *L. j.* 'Aureo-reticulata' is a well-behaved, short Japanese honeysuckle. It is called the gold-net honeysuckle, and is prized for its small, roundish leaves with bright yellow veins. I grow it at the base of a once-blooming climbing rose, and it lights up the area. It has never flowered in the 4 years I've grown it. There are many members of the genus *Lonicera* that are not vines, but we will not discuss them here.

Cultural Information: The honeysuckles make very few demands on the gardener, and are tolerant of drought and shade. They flourish in ordinary soils, even in poor and heavy soils. They should be pruned back to encourage branching or to keep them to a particular size. It is best to prune in fall right after they stop flowering. In the North, they may be pruned in early spring before they leaf out.

Love-in-a-puff; see ***Cardiospermum***

Madagascar jasmine; see ***Stephanotis***

Mandevilla (man-de-VILL-a)
Mandevilla splendens, **dipladenia, pink allamanda;** ***Mandevilla laxa,*** **Chilean jasmine;** TP, F, E, ○ ◑
Zones: 8 to 10
Height: 20 to 30 feet
Colors: Pink, white
Characteristics: Dipladenia's (*Mandevilla sanderi*) long-lasting, trumpet-shaped flowers grow in clusters of soft shades of pink or white. Each flower reaches 5 inches long and flares to 2 to 4 inches wide. The plants flower from April to November when grown in pots, and almost year 'round if grown outdoors in frost-free areas. Their dark green, oval, leathery leaves are 3 to 8 inches long. Dipladenia is a slow grower with a chubby shape until it ages some. However, it blooms even when small in a 4-inch pot. It produces long, climbing stems and sparse foliage that may reach 15 feet. It grows faster in the ground than in a container, where it may not need pruning for several years. For the container gardener, slow growth can be a plus; slow-growing plants seldom need repotting or pruning. Prune dipladenia right after the plant stops flowering, because each year's flowers are produced on new growth, so if you prune out the new stems you won't have flowers the following summer. Dipladenia can be trained to grow on a wire hoop or small trellis. Indoors, it needs warm temperatures (60° F.) and humid air. Misting, or setting the pot in a saucer filled with gravel and water, helps keep the atmosphere around it moist. *Mandevilla laxa,* a native of Argentina, is hardy to

Mandevilla splendens *can be grown in a pot indoors in the North, where it can summer outdoors on terraces.*

Zone 8, grows to 15 feet high and has 2-inch-long, funnel-shaped, white flowers that emit a wonderful, sweet fragrance.

Cultural Information: Dipladema prefers a rich soil. When growing it outdoors, supplement the soil with compost, or well-rotted or dehydrated cow manure. Liquid fertilize container-grown plants regularly, following the package directions. Provide a frame for the vine to grow on when you plant it. Pinch back stems on young vines to induce bushiness. It is tolerant of salt air. Check for spider mites.

Maurandia; see *Asarina*

Mile-a-minute vine; see *Po-lygonum*

Mina (MEYE-na) **Mina lo-bata (formerly Qua-moclit lobata, Ipomoea versicolor), crimson star-glory,** A and P, E (as peren-nial), ○
Zone: 10
Height: 4 to 6 feet
Colors: Scarlet, yellow, orange
Characteristics: Mina lobata, a vigorous, climbing perennial from Mexico, is often grown as an annual. The first time I saw it, it was used as the focal point in a long flower border. Grown on the 4-foot-high tripod set closer to the front than the back of the border, it was the tallest flower. It was arresting. Each flower is boat shaped. The fiery scarlet buds open to creamy yellow and orange, so all the colors of the sunset are glowing on the vine when it blooms at summer's end.
Cultural Information: An an-nual easy to grow from seed, crimson starglory should be grown as often as morning glo-ries are. The culture is similar to that for morning glories (see *Ipomoea*). The seeds can be started indoors in March and moved outdoors in May after the soil has warmed. They may be direct sown outdoors after all danger of frost is past and the soil has warmed.

Moonflower; see *Ipomoea*

Mina lobata *twines a 4-foot-high tripod to bloom at summer's end in the middle of a flower border.*

Virginia creeper (Parthenocissus quinquefolia) *grows and climbs easily almost any wall with its adhesive tendril tips.*

Morning glory; see *Ipomoea*

Nasturtium; see *Tropaeo-lum*

Oriental bittersweet; see *Cel-astrus*

Paper flower; see *Bougain-villea*

Paradise flower; see *Sola-num*

Parthenocissus (par-thee-no-SISS-us) **Parthenocissus quinquefolia,** **Virginia creeper, woodbine,** P, D, ○ ◐ ●
Zones: 3 to 9
Height: 40 or more feet
Color: Green foliage turns fiery in fall
Characteristics: Virginia creeper is especially loved for its fall foliage—the entire vine changes color and the leaves glow bright orange to scarlet. The fan-shaped leaves are com-posed of 5 separate leaflets, each 6 inches long with saw-toothed edges. This is a vigor-ous vine that can control ero-sion when grown on a slope. It can be invasive, crowding out other plants in a small garden. The inconspicuous flowers pro-duce bluish-black berries loved by birds. The new growth is red and decorative. Virginia creeper is a rapid grower that climbs by attaching itself to an upright-surface using adhesive discs on tendril tips. Once established it is difficult to eliminate. It has the ability to grow in seemingly impossible situations. A firm pruning hand will keep it in bounds, but if a year of pruning is skipped, look out. 'Engel-mannii' is a variety with

smaller leaves and denser growth.

Cultural Information: Not particularly fussy about soil, Virginia creeper grows easily almost anywhere. It needs only moderate feeding. Don't plant it to grow on shingle siding, as it can creep under the shingles and it is hard to remove for painting. It is resistant to disease and insects.

Parthenocissus (par-thee-no-SISS-us) *Parthenocissus tricuspidata,* **Boston ivy, Japanese creeper, Japanese ivy,** P, SE, ○ ◑ ●

Zones: 4 to 9
Height: 60 feet
Color: Red fall foliage
Characteristics: Boston ivy is the cover of choice for college buildings, and is the source of the expression "Ivy League." The Boston ivy that covers the walls of Princeton was planted by the class of 1866, and it still looks great today. Adhesive discs bind it to brick, stone, trees or any other surface on which the plants form a dense, even covering. Without the help of a trellis or guidance from the gardener, they will blanket the ground. The glossy green leaves, shaped like maple leaves, each consist of 3 leaflets up to 8 inches wide; mature plants may produce a mixture of foliage shapes including single, heart-shaped leaves and 3-lobed leaves. Older vines have inconspicuous flowers and blue-black berries that are enjoyed by the birds. Birds frequently build nests in the ivy on the sides of buildings.

'Lowii' has smaller (1½-inch), deeply cut, crinkled leaves. 'Veitchii' has smaller leaves that turn purple in autumn. 'Green Showers' has large leaves that turn burgundy in fall. Boston ivy is a naturalized citizen, not a native American. It comes from Japan and central China.

Cultural Information: Faster growing and hardier than English ivy, Boston ivy is one of the easiest ivies to grow, tolerating shade, pollution and drought. It is adaptable to most sites and exposures, and requires only ample water and moderate feeding.

Passiflora (pass-i-FLO-ra) *Passiflora caerulea,* **blue crown passion flower;** *Passiflora incarnata,* **maypop;** *Passiflora vitifolia,* **red passion flower;** *Passiflora × alatocaerulea;* TP, F; E, SE, or D; ○ ◑

Zones: 8 to 9
Height: 20 to 30 feet
Colors: Purple, red
Characteristics: The passion flower received its name from Spanish explorers in Brazil, missionaries who thought they saw symbols of the crucifixion in the wonderful blooms. The 10 petals were thought to represent the 10 apostles present at Christ's death (Peter and Judas being absent). The anthers represent the wounds, and the stigma, the nails. The delicately fringed corona resembles the crown of thorns or halo. The 5-lobed leaves represent the hands of the persecutors, and the tendrils, the whips and cords used.

Boston ivy (Parthenocissus tricuspidata) *softens the outline of any building with dense green leaves. It is at its best when it turns fiery red in the fall (see page 20).*

The red passionflower (Passiflora vitifolia) *has decorative red bracts at the base of each flower that stay after the flowers fall.*

Passiflora caerulea is a popular vine in southern and southwestern gardens. It is a popular houseplant or greenhouse plant in the North.

Passion flower is grown commercially for its fragrance, and it is used in making perfume. It flowers singly or in pairs from June to September. A striking feature is the single or double row of filaments, or corona, at the base of the flower. The fruit is edible, about the size of a plum with a thick, leathery, deep purple hull. The fruits are said to have the combined flavor of peach, apricot, pineapple, guava, banana, lemon and lime. Fruits are never picked from the vine, but are gathered from the ground, where they fall when ripe. Fragrant golden pulp sacs contain edible black seeds and fill the fruit. The vines are the favorite food of the caterpillars of the Gulf fritillary butterfly.

Passiflora caerulea is easy to grow under most conditions. It is a popular vine often used in southern and southwestern gardens, tolerating heat, coastal conditions, and semiarid and arid atmospheres. Not only does it flourish outdoors, but it is quite often grown as a houseplant or greenhouse plant. The red passion flower (*P. vitifolia*) is a rich deep crimson. This tropical vine has decorative bracts at the base of each flower. After the faded flowers drop, the bracts make the vine handsome still. Native to the eastern United States, maypop (*P. incarnata*) is frequently found growing along roadsides and in fields from Virginia to Florida. It spreads prodigiously by root runners. Its 1½- to 2-inch-wide flowers bear 5 white petals. In the center of each is a crown of purple and white filaments. The 2-inch fruit is yellow, egg-shaped and edible. It is easily grown from seed. Passion vines are good at holding the soil when grown on a slope as a groundcover. They can be pruned anytime, but prune judiciously as they usually bud at the tips.

Cultural Information: Best results are obtained when these plants are grown in full sun, but they tolerate partial shade, and wind. Mature vines will stand temperatures to 28° F. They are rampant growers; do not plant them in a confined area, but rather in outlying areas of the garden. A neutral soil (pH 7) is best. Soil should be deep, moist, well-drained, sandy loam, containing lots of organic matter. Equal parts of loam, sand, peat moss and leaf mold is ideal. Passion flower must be fertilized and watered properly. Well-rotted barnyard manures may be used. During periods of very hot, dry weather, you may need to water regularly. Keep the soil evenly moist. It is most important to provide a sturdy lattice or trellis. Vigorous plants are likely to overgrow and tangle, so good supports for the tendrils to cling to are important. When grown in pots indoors by windows, use bamboo stakes and attach strings against the windows so that the tendrils may take hold.

Pruning is essential to keep the plants growing vigorously. Prune heavily annually once the vines are 2 years old, to thin them and keep them under control. The plant should be pinched back as it grows, to encourage a more branched vine. Passion flower makes an excellent winter houseplant. During the early winter, the plants need a rest period, so provide a temperature of 55° F. and keep them on the dry side. In late winter increase the temperature by 15° to 20° F. and give the plants more water. It may be necessary to repot the plant if blooming slows considerably and the roots fill the pot. Feed every 2 to 3 weeks year 'round with a mild solution of flowering houseplant fertilizer. Passion flower is almost immune to pests.

Passion flower; see ***Passiflora***

Phaseolus (fass-EE-o-lus)
Phaseolus coccineus,
scarlet runner bean, A, ○

Height: 15 feet
Color: Scarlet
Characteristics: Scarlet runner beans arrived in North America with the pilgrims, who valued them for their foot-long pods of edible beans. Today scarlet runner bean is more often grown as an ornamental for its clusters of brilliant scarlet flowers. Everything about this vine is attractive, the foliage, flowers and seedpods. There are improved varieties available for eating, although none of these is as attractive growing on a fence or trellis. The vines grow quickly and easily, flowering and producing beans continuously all summer until heavy frost.
Cultural Information: Add compost, well-rotted manure, peat or other humus to improve your soil. If you are growing scarlet runner beans in the vegetable garden, plant them at the north end so they don't shade smaller plants. Set the supports in place before planting the seeds, so you don't risk damaging the plants or their roots later.

Plant in spring after all danger of frost is past and after the soil has become warm. Sown in cool soil, bean seeds are very susceptible to rot. Because beans attract their own source of nitrogen fertilizer, they need less nitrogen fertilizer during growth than most vegetables. Excessive application of manure or other fertilizers high in nitrogen will stimulate growth but reduce yields of flowers

Scarlet runner bean (Phaseolus coccineus) *is both decorative and edible.*

and beans. Remember: Beans put nitrogen back into the soil, and should be rotated where lettuces, squashes and members of the mustard family have been grown, preferably the previous year, because these crops lower the nitrogen content of the soil. At season's end, till or dig in the bean stalks. They will further improve your soil as they decompose over the winter. Beans require that nitrogen-fixing bacteria be present in soil, so the addition of legume inoculant is essential. Beans generally do not transplant well and should be sown where they are to grow. If started indoors, they are best grown in peat pots that can be planted directly into the ground without disturbing the roots.

Pink allamanda; see ***Mandevilla***

Plumbago capensis has clear blue flowers that grow profusely much of the year in tropical climates.

Pipe vine; see ***Aristolochia***

Plumbago (plum-BAY-go)
Plumbago capensis,
Cape plumbago, TP, E, ○ ◑

Zones: 9 and 10
Height: 15 or more feet
Colors: Light blue, white
Characteristics: A popular shrub in Florida for foundation plantings, plumbago is easily grown as a vine. It sends out long shoots that can be tied to a support or a wall. The long, tubed flowers bloom in round, phloxlike clusters and are profuse much of the year in tropical climates. The clear light blue flowers (a color that goes well with everything) show to great advantage against its yellow-green foliage. There is a white variety, 'Alba', available, but the blue is so beautiful it

would be a shame not to grow it. This is an easy vine to grow in a container in northern gardens; it should be taken indoors before frost, where it will bloom from March to December. Grown outdoors, plumbago blooms almost all year 'round. During cold winters in northern Florida it can be killed to the ground, but usually it will recover. Elongated, burrlike capsules form after the flowers.

Cultural Information: Grow plumbago in enriched soil, and water well until it is established. It will adapt to poor soil and, once established, to drought as well. Hot sun can fade the color of the blossoms. Propagate from cuttings or grow from seed. If grown from seed, the color may vary from white to various light blues. In selecting plants at a nursery, it is best to buy a pot already in flower to see precisely what color you are getting.

Poison ivy; see *Rhus*

Polygonum (po-LIG-on-um)
***Polygonum aubertii*,** **fleece vine, silverlace vine, mile-a-minute vine, P, F, D, ○ ◑**

Zones: 4 to 9
Height: 30 to 40 feet
Color: White
Characteristics: A native of Tibet and China, the silverlace vine heads for the skies with the speed of a rocket, so plant it and stand back for the countdown. Once it takes off, you can clip its wings yearly, or plant it in order to cover an ugly structure—a chain link fence or outbuilding—and let it

Silverlace vine (Polygonum aubertii) *may grow more than 15 feet the first season.*

take over entirely. Depending on how early in spring it is planted, and the length of the growing season, it may grow more than 15 feet tall the first year (sometimes as much as 20 or 25); if grown on the ground it can cover 100 square feet in a season. This vine is a good choice to screen an unsightly view, or to cover a large expanse of fence beautifully and in the fastest time possible. It clings to any support without harming it and provides huge, billowing sprays of white, summer flowers. If the vines are not pruned back, the flowers start in June; otherwise, they appear at summer's end. The vines can be pruned to the ground yearly to keep them within bounds. Fleece vine's glossy, heart-shaped leaves have wavy edges and are from 1½ to 2 inches long.

Cultural Information: Fleece vine is not particular about soil as long as it is moist and well drained. Water deeply at least monthly. Too rich a soil can result in excessively coarse growth. It is not bothered by salt air. Pruning in late winter or early spring is best to contain growth and shape.

Porcelain vine; see *Ampelopsis*

Potato vine; see *Solanum*

Pueraria (PEW-ra) *Pueraria lobata*, kudzu vine, P, F, D, ○ ◑ ●

Zones: 6 to 10
Height: 75 feet and more
Color: Green foliage
Characteristics: Along the expressway south of Atlanta, Georgia, kudzu leaps up to the tallest trees, draping over them and weaving them all together to form what appear (from a distance) to be prehistoric monsters. Growing as much as a foot a day, kudzu is the fastest-growing woody vine in the temperate United States. It propagates readily from seeds, cuttings and roots. Kudzu has no natural enemies in this country and smothers everything in its path, preventing sunlight from reaching other plants, and devouring their nutrients and water underground.

Kudzu was introduced in this country in 1876 as a "miracle" intended to solve many of the country's agricultural problems. Instead, it has become known as "the vine that ate the South." At the turn of the century it was planted extensively there to decorate porches and provide shade. Its beautiful, dense foliage hides the fragrant, violet-purple, beanlike flowers. As early as 1902, warnings about its invasive nature were issued by botanist David Fairchild, but they went unheeded. By 1934 an estimated 10,000 acres of kudzu was in cultivation for use as livestock pasturage and fodder. Yet even after 20 years of research with kudzu, the United States government ignored its invasive nature, recommending it as an erosion control, soil amendment and cattle feed, and offering assistance payments of up to $8 for each acre of kudzu planted. David Fairchild again published warnings about kudzu in 1938, but 73 million more kudzu seedlings were planted along highways by 1940. The Kudzu Club of America was founded in Atlanta in 1943, and "Kudzu: Another Agricultural Miracle," appeared in *Reader's Digest* in 1945. It wasn't until 1954 that the USDA removed kudzu from its recommended list of cover crops, and in 1960 shifted its focus to eradication research. Finally it was recognized as too much of a good thing. (Recently a *New York Times* article mentioned research on kudzu in connection with treatment for alcoholism, treatment that is used extensively in China and is being tested here.)

Looking back over kudzu's history in this country, it is hard to understand how we could have gone so wrong, unless you consider its good points. Kudzu is not invasive in its native Japan. All parts of the high-fiber, protein-rich plant are edible, and it is popular in many recipes as well as in medicines. It grows even in drought, which adds to the problems in America, but makes it valuable for grazing stock animals in Japan. A member of the bean family, it returns nitrogen to the soil and will improve soil condition, especially if the plants are tilled back into the soil. In Japan, paper, fabric and baskets are made from the vine. Kudzu

Kudzu (Pueraria lobata) *has been called "the vine that ate the South." It kills trees and shrubs by covering them and preventing sunlight from reaching their leaves.*

baskets are now made in the United States.

Controlling kudzu is not easy. Along the highways herbicides are used. In other areas it is killed naturally by planned overgrazing of cattle and by continuous mowing. If kudzu is a problem where you live, contact your local extension agent for the safest method of eradication. For more information, contact the Education Department at Callaway Gardens, Pine Mountain, GA 31822-2000, or see Shurleff and Aoyagi, *The Book of Kudzu*, New Jersey: Avery Press, 1985.
Cultural Information: Kudzu adapts to any soil and weather conditions. There is no natural enemy in North America to keep it in check. Unfortunately, it is still being sold in garden catalogues and nurseries. Please, don't buy it or plant it.

Purple bell vine (Rhodochiton) *holds its flowers for 6 to 8 weeks.*

Purple bell vine; see Rhodochiton

Red passion flower; see *Passiflora*

Rhodochiton (ro-do-CHIT-on) ***Rhodochiton atrosanguiineum,* purple bell vine,** TP, A, ○ ◐
Zones: 9 to 10
Height: 10 to 15 feet
Color: Purple
Characteristics: Rhodochiton's purple bells hang on thin stems that look like fishing lines for 6 to 8 weeks. Each individual "flower" is formed by a calyx, the outer layer of floral leaves, only an inch across. Inside the bell is the real flower, a one-inch-long, deep red-purple (almost black) and gong-shape, that gradually grows longer, swelling as it produces seeds. When the seeds are ripe, it opens to release them, and stays open inside the calyx to

form a bell within a bell. The calyx remains long after the seeds have been dispersed, making the vine ornamental for several weeks longer. The leaves are heart-shaped. Purple bell vine climbs by clasping leaf stems. If grown in a sunny window or a greenhouse, it will bloom year 'round. Grown outdoors as an annual, it blooms as long as the weather is warm (with day temperatures of 70° F. and above). Gardeners in the North grow purple bell vine, originally from Mexico, in hanging baskets and as houseplants in 5- or 6-inch pots. In San Francisco at Strybing Arboretum, it is grown up the base of a tree.
Cultural Information: When grown as an annual, purple bell vine is best started indoors in February. The seeds should be lightly covered, and will germinate in approximately 2 weeks at temperatures of 70° F. Grow in peat pots with a sterile potting soil that is kept moist, but not soggy. The seeds are fairly easy to grow, and with continued warmth the plants should bloom in approximately 4 months. They can only be transplanted outdoors when days have warmed to 60° F. Purple bell vine prefers a south-facing wall or a sheltered corner; even if there is no danger of frost, the vine won't grow well without heat. If the vine is to grow up, provide a support and help it by tying it up. I prefer to see the wispy stems trail from a hanging basket. Grown this way, the roots are restricted and the vine will grow shorter, 4 to 5 feet, the perfect size.

Poison ivy contains a nonvolatile oil throughout the plant that causes an allergic skin reaction in most people. The plant can be identified by the way it holds three leaves together.

Rhus (RUSS) ***Rhus radicans,*** **poison ivy,** P, D, ○ ◐ ●
Zones: 5
Height: 30 or more feet
Color: Red leaves in spring and autumn
Characteristics: The children's chant, "leaflets three, let it be," is well known to those who live where poison ivy grows. This noxious native of eastern North America has a resin or nonvolatile oil in its roots, leaves, stems, hairs and berries that causes an allergic skin reaction in most people, usually redness and itching followed by swelling and blisters. The oil is potent even in dead plants and dormant roots. Worse, if the vine is burned, the oil becomes even more dangerous as it is vaporized in the air. When inhaled, it can irritate the lungs as well as the skin. I know of

one unlucky flower arranger who gathered the brown, twisted stems for a winter wreath, mistakenly thinking it was grape vine, and developed a terrible case of poison ivy.

The easiest time to identify and eradicate the vines is in spring when the new, red, shiny leaves are easy to spot. The oval, pointed leaves grow in threes, and turn green when a few weeks old. Wear heavy gloves and clothing from head to toe for digging and pulling out the roots. I don't recommend using toxic chemicals, as they stay in the soil. In my own garden, every plant that grew in the contaminated soil where I had killed poison ivy was stunted and discolored, and this didn't change until I replaced the soil. Poison ivy is deciduous, turning a beautiful red in autumn before the leaves fall. It produces berries from late August through November, small, yellow and fleshy, each containing one stony seed. The fruit is eaten by birds that carry and drop the seeds in new locations. Thanks to birds, I have found poison ivy growing even in the raised beds in my vegetable garden. Poison ivy is invasive, spreading by underground runners. The vines climb with clinging aerial roots and frequently slither up tree trunks. Poison ivy's woody trunk thickens as it ages and produces no leaves along its bottom half to give it away.

Cultural Information: This is obviously not a recommended plant, but rather, one that should be eradicated in home gardens. A number of soaps act as a preventive to the rash and may be used immediately after exposure to poison ivy. Tecnu is a liquid soap that washes the oil off your skin up to 6 hours after exposure; it is the most effective product I have found for preventing a rash or keeping it from spreading.

Rosa (RO-sa) *Rosa* in variety, **climbing roses**, P, F (many available), D, ○

Zones: All
Height: 6 to 30 or more feet, depending on variety
Colors: Red, pink, apricot, yellow, white, bicolors
Characteristics: Roses don't really climb—at least, not as vines do, with clinging tendrils, supple twining stems or aerial roots to pull them up. Roses have long, awkward canes. Most climbing and rambler roses sprawl, arch, creep and scramble over the ground, stretching out long stems. None will do exactly as you wish, and all are like wayward children, needing guidance. Successful climbers must be watched during periods of quick growth so you see what they want to do and learn to work with them. To grow up, roses must be secured to latticework, a pillar, a fence, a trellis, an arch, a porch or the side of a building. Because they travel straight up, the feet of climbing roses are exposed to the drying sun. They need shade on their roots, which is why they do well as a backdrop to a flower border; the "bordering" flowers shade their roots.

Climbing roses, thankful for a place on a warm wall, smile down from their height, and it is impossible not to smile back.

On the author's back arbor, three climbing roses twine together: pink 'Aloha', yellow 'Golden Showers', and orange and yellow 'Joseph's Coat'. 'Simplicity', a shrub rose, is in the foreground.

They are cordial characters, combining easily with other plants, and they should be planted more often. Ramblers, climbing roses with longer canes, are seldom seen today, but they are worth seeking out as nothing else can so regally enrobe a house. The flirtatious ramblers sprawl and flaunt their blooms, and they must be coaxed into appropriate behavior. Show them the way, and they will surprise you with their ingenuity. One 'American Pillar' rose I planted to cover a chimney did much more than

Rosa *'Golden Showers' will spread her wings quite a distance when lightly pruned. Clematis 'Romona' climbs her bare legs.*

Climbing Rosa *'Margo Koster' has small, uniquely globe-shaped coral flowers that bloom in clusters.*

that. It did cover the chimney, then sent one cane around the corner to create a sweeping floral hanging on the other side. I couldn't have planned a prettier effect myself. Our house was clothed in ivy, and the rose clung to it and wandered wherever it wished. The rambler 'Lady Banks' is one rose nicknamed "house-eater," precisely for this proclivity to climb up a roof and dangle flowers over the other side. The best climbers for a bold display are those that bloom but once a season. Frequently they wait until their second year to bloom, and they bloom best on the previous year's growth.

"Rambler" is applied to roses with stems that grow 10 to 20 feet a year, usually with dense clusters of small flowers, each up to 2 inches across. They require good air circulation, as they are susceptible to mildew. Many varieties spend all their energy their first year in reaching upwards, and pro-

duce few or no blooms until the following year. Some of the wilder, longer varieties arch so high they catch on the lower branches of trees, then send up new branches that reach up even farther into the tree. Most often ramblers bloom once in late spring or early summer on year-old canes. Their colors range from pinks through red, peach, yellow and white.

Climbing hybrid teas are the result of a "sport" or unusually long-stemmed bush that is selected to be grown as a climber. In many cases they have fewer flowers and are not as hardy as the hybrid tea from which they were derived. Pillar roses are not as long-stemmed as other climbing roses, but they grow more upright, with tall, straight, stiffer stems that reach from 5 to 10 feet. They're named pillar roses because they are often planted beside and tied to a lamp post, one of the supports of an arbor, a flag pole, a telephone pole or a fence post. The rose decorates the pillar, and the pillar protects the rose's long canes from wind damage.

Roses are a complicated and diverse group of plants. There are whole books devoted solely to them, including one in the Burpee American Gardening Series, where you will find detailed information readily available.

Cultural Information: A rose well planted is on its way to being well grown. Don't take a short cut. Good soil preparation makes the difference between a healthy rose and a rose susceptible to disease. Most roses are voracious feeders and need enriched soil. A rose grown in poor, lean soil will lose its beauty. Ideally the pH should be between 6.0 and 6.8. Give new3 roses the best possible soil in order to prepare them for a long, happy, healthy life.

Bare-root roses are available through the mail or from nurseries early in the season. They are less expensive than container-grown roses, and it is easy to train their roots to grow into your garden's soil. Container-grown roses are easier to plant, but beware of rose "bargains" late in the planting season; many times such roses have been in their pots too long. Their roots, ingrown and warped, are unable to grow out into the soil in search of nutrients. Stunted roots produce stunted canes with few flowers.

Check bare-root roses to see if any of the roots are broken or damaged; if so, cut off the problem area. Cut back the dark areas at the end of the canes by a few inches, and remove any damaged canes. If any canes appear to be crisscrossed, cut one or both out. As soon as you receive a bare-root rose, submerge the entire plant in a bucket of warm water for a minimum of 24 hours and a maximum of 72 hours. Deprived of soil during shipping, it has been dehydrated. Adding a polymer to the soaking water will help prevent transplant shock. The polymers will adhere to the roots and keep moisture readily available when the bush is planted, helping to reduce transplant shock.

Dig a hole 24 inches deep and several inches wider than the circumference of the roots or root ball. The hole should be large enough for the planted rose to be surrounded on all sides by well-supplemented, nutritious soil. Depending on your type of soil and the amount of preparation previously done in the bed, add approximately one-half to equal amounts of a mix of compost, peat moss and/or well-rotted manure to the soil dug from the hole. All three additives will improve the structure of the soil, and in addition, manure and compost add nutrients. At the very least, work in dried cow manure and peat moss because you are preparing this hole for a lifetime of growth, and the rose needs the best possible start. For bare-root roses, shape the soil at the bottom of the hole in an inverted cone. The roots of roses grow out from the bud union, where you can detect the graft. Plant the rose so the bud union sis on top of the cone of soil. The rose's roots will be supported by the cone's sides. The roots must be spread out evenly and pointed down. The bud union should sit aboveground in southern climates, level with the ground where winters are mild, and an inch or two lower in colder, northern areas. Place a stick across the hole to help you see where the bud union is in relation to the ground level. If the rose doesn't have a bud union, plant it with the roots and 1 inch of the main cane underground. Remember that if the soil has been recently prepared and hasn't been allowed to settle, it will compact somewhat, so more soil may have to be added later to assure the bud union is planted at the proper depth. For a container-grown rose, the hole and the soil should be prepared the same way, but without the cone-shaped pile of soil. Gently release the roots from the soil to help them grow out into the new soil and not wind around into themselves. The roots, soil and all, are placed in the hole with the bud union at the proper level, as described above.

Fill the hole with the remaining soil and firm it in place by gently stepping around the bush. Add a slow-release fertilizer, well-rotted manure and Epsom salts (see "Fertilizers," page 31). Mound a rim of soil 6 to 8 inches high around the edge of the hole to protect the bud union from wind, and to hold water. Water with a gentle trickle until the hole is full and water starts to run down the sides of the soil rim. If you are planting early and a chance of cold, harsh weather is still possible, mound the soil up around the canes to a height of 8 inches. This will warm them and protect them from drying winds until the weather warms and growth can begin. Always water new rose bushes thoroughly at the time of planting.

Royal jasmine; see *Jasminum*

Scarlet runner bean; see *Phaseolus*

CLIMBING ROSES

Rose	Color	Size of Blooms	Fragrance	Height	Blooming	Uses
'Aloha'	mp	3½ inches wide, double (55–60 petals)	FF	7 to 10 feet	R	Pillar, trellis
'America'	op (c/s)	3½ to 4½ inches wide, double (40–45 petals)	FF	9 to 12 feet tall	R	Trellis
'American Pillar'	dp	2 to 4 inches wide, single (5–7 petals)		15 to 20 feet	O	Trellis, gazebo
'Blaze'	mr	2½ to 3 inches wide, semidouble (15–20 petals)	F	8 to 15 feet	R	Fence, trellis
'Constance Spry'	lp	4½ to 5 inches wide, double (45–55 petals)	FF	6 to 7 feet	O	Climbing, shrub, landscape, back of the border, also disease resistant
'Don Juan'	dr	4½ to 5 inches wide, double (35 petals)	FF	6 to 10 feet	R	Trellis, pillar
'Eden'	pb	3 inches wide, quartered (100 or more petals)	FF	6 to 8 feet		Fence, trellis
'Golden Showers'	my	3 to 4 inches wide, double (20–35 petals)	F	6 to 12 feet	R	Fence, trellis
'Joseph's Coat'	rb	3 to 4 inches wide, double (24–30 petals)	F	6 to 10 feet	R	Landscaping, fence, trellis
'New Dawn'	lp	2 to 3½ inches wide, semidouble (18–24 petals)	F	12 to 20 feet	R	Pillar, trellis, wall
'Red Cascade'	dr	1½ inches wide, double (35 petals)	F	6 to 20 feet	R	Hanging basket, hedge, bank, groundcover, pillar
'Zéphirine Drouhin'	mp	2 to 4 inches wide, semidouble (15–20 petals)	F	8 to 15 feet	C	Pillar, climbing into a tree, trellis, wall

FRAGRANCE: *Fragrance may be slight (F) or moderate (FF). Remember that the fragrance of a rose changes with the weather and the length of time the rose has been in bloom.*

COLOR: *The color classifications used are as defined by the American Rose Society; where I don't agree with the designated color, I have added my interpretation in parentheses:*

ab	apricot and apricot blend
dp	deep pink
dr	dark red
dy	deep yellow
lp	light pink
ly	light yellow
m	mauve and mauve blend
mp	medium pink
mr	medium red
my	medium yellow
op	orange-pink (c/s coral-salmon)
or	orange-red
ob	orange and orange blend
pb	pink blend
r	russet
rb	red blend
w	white or near white
yb	yellow blend

BLOOMING: *Once-a-year bloomers (O) bloom once a season for a 3- to 4-week period. Many old roses are in this category. Repeat bloomers (R) bloom heavily in spring, with perhaps a few blooms over the summer, and then a full, but not as heavy bloom in the fall. Continuous bloomers (C) include many modern roses, such as the hybrid teas, that bloom modestly but continuously for many months.*

FLOWER SIZE AND DESCRIPTION: *The size of the flowers varies with the rose's diet and growing conditions. Most roses have larger flowers at the beginning of the bloom season. The following explains the flower descriptions:*

Single	4 to 7 petals in a single row
Semidouble	12 to 24 petals in two rows
Double	more than 25 overlapping petals in three or more rows
Quartered	so many petals tucked into a cup shape that the petals stand straight up and are flattened against each other. The petals form a scalloped arrangement, dividing the flower into four equal parts. The top of the flower is so flat that it appears to have been sliced off across the top with a sharp knife.

The flowers of Solanum dulcamara *bloom all summer and have the look of bright, blue-purple shooting stars falling to earth.*

Solanum wendlandii, *the Costa Rican nightshade, has pale lilac flowers 2½ inches across.*

Shining jasmine; see *Jasminum*

Silverlace vine; see *Polygonum*

Solanum (so-LAY-num) *Solanum jasminoides,* potato vine, jasmine nightshade; *Solanum dulcamara,* bittersweet, woody nightshade, bitter nightshade; *Solanum wendlandii,* Costa Rican nightshade, potato vine, paradise flower; P and A, E and D, ○

Zones: 5 to 10
Height: to 30 feet
Colors: White, bluish white, blue-purple, purple
Characteristics: The nightshade family (*Solanaceae*) contains more than 1,700 species and includes eggplant and potatoes. The woody nightshade, or bittersweet (*S. dulcamara*), is not to be confused with the quite different American bittersweet (*Celastrus*). This hardy vine from Europe and Asia has naturalized in North America. The flowers bloom all summer and have the look of bright, blue-purple shooting stars falling to earth; they hang in clusters with their petals curved back over their heads and their showy yellow stamens facing down. Later, the vine is covered with ½-inch-long oval berries in bright green clusters that ripen to scarlet. The vine can climb to 15 feet, but more often spreads along the ground, under which its roots spread most rapidly underground. It can become a weedy nuisance. All parts of this vine are poisonous if eaten raw.

The annual potato vine or jasmine nightshade is an import from Brazil. With slender stems, it is very decorative when covered with its starry white or bluish-white flowers with yellow stamens. The flowers grow in clusters of 8 to 12. The leaves are lance-shaped and 1 to 3 inches long. The vines can grow 20 to 30 feet, and bloom from midsummer until frost. Flowering is heaviest in spring, but nearly perpetual in frost-free areas. Potato vine is perennial in Zones 9 and 10, and it can recover from chilly periods that may cause it to lose its usually evergreen leaves. It can be slightly pruned or cut back severely at any time to control its rampant runners, remove tangles or promote new growth.

The Costa Rican nightshade is deciduous. It is a coarser and wilder cousin, growing to 50 feet, but surviving winters only in Zone 10. Its flowers are larger, 2½ inches across, and a pale lilac-blue color. Its stems are prickly, and the leaves are large, 4 to 10 inches long. This vine can climb tall trees or cover an arbor.

It is best to assume all of these vines are poisonous because it is hard to tell which of them are harmless.

Cultural Information: Although potato vines are adaptable and easy to grow, sunny spots with a southern or western exposure are the best places to grow them. They are not particular about soil, and they are easily grown from seeds or cuttings planted out in spring. As they are all fast growers, put supports in place at planting time. The vines are pruned as they grow. This encourages branching and a taller vine.

Star jasmine; see **Trachelospermum**

Stephanotis (steff-an-O-tis) **Stephanotis floribunda,** stephanotis, Madagascar jasmine, TP, F, E, ○ ◑

Zone: 10
Height: 15 feet
Color: White
Characteristics: A favorite flower of brides, stephanotis announces a wedding with its heavy, sweet perfume and clusters of trumpet-shaped flowers. The individual flowers are 2 inches long, with thick, waxy petals. It is a slow-growing, tropical vine that blooms from spring to early fall. The flowers are long lasting both on the vine and as cut flowers. The thick, glossy, deep green leaves grow to 4 inches long and are the perfect complement to the bright white flowers. Stephantotis is most often grown in a greenhouse or, pruned to a smaller size, on a sunny windowsill. It can be kept small through pruning. Grown outdoors, it blooms all summer. Indoors, it requires a period of dormancy during which it is kept drier and fertilizer is withheld. It will rebloom approximately 6 weeks after it resumes its growth.
Cultural Information: Grown outdoors, stephanotis needs protection from the sun and

benefits from a location in partial shade. The soil should be rich in organic matter, moist yet well-drained. If growing indoors, use a sterile potting soil and keep the soil evenly moist, fertilizing monthly at half strength. Withhold fertilizer during the winter to give the plant a rest. Ideal temperatures for bloom are pleasant nights of 60° to 65° F. and warmer days of 70° F. and above. Indoors, stephanotis needs a minimum of 4 hours of direct sunlight, though it prefers its roots in shade. If summer sun is intense, the pot can be placed where it will receive filtered sunlight to prevent the leaves from scouring. New plants can be propagated from seeds or cuttings. Occasionally, stephanotis is attacked by scale and mealybugs.

Sweet pea; see **Lathyrus**

Thunbergia (thun-BER-ja) **Thunbergia alata,** black-eyed Susan vine, clockvine; **Thunbergia grandiflora;** TP, A, NA, ○ ◑
Zones: Black-eyed Susan vine, 10; *T. grandiflora,* 8 to 10
Height: 8 to 10 feet
Colors: White, buff, yellow or orange petals with dark eyes
Characteristics: The flowers of black-eyed Susan vine resemble the wild daisies with the same common name. This delightful little climber has 3-inch-long, arrowhead-shaped leaves, and round, 1- to 2-inch-wide flowers with contrasting purple-black throats. A versatile vine, it is tall enough to look good climbing up a picket fence and short enough to hang down from a window box or hanging basket. It can even be left to sprawl as a groundcover, or grown as a houseplant in

Stephanotis floribunda *is a favorite flower of brides.*

Black-eyed Susan vine (Thunbergia alata) *is at home in a hanging basket.*

winter on a sunny window ledge. It is a perennial vine in the tropics, but is grown as an annual everywhere else. It is light enough to grow on strings or a trellis. 'Susie' (mixed colors) is a good choice for a hanging basket. *T. grandiflora*, a native of India, blooms nearly year 'round with sky blue, 3-inch-long flowers with contrasting yellow throats.

Cultural Information: Thunbergia prefers a light, rich, moist, well-drained soil. It does not like excessive heat, preferring night temperatures of 50° to 60° F. and higher day temperatures, though below 72° F. It needs only moderate humidity; high humidity causes fungus diseases. Repot when roots become crowded, but do not prune during the growing season. When growing it as a houseplant or in a container, lightly fertilize with 7-6-19 on a monthly basis when in active growth. Prune after flowering to the size appropriate for the pot. *Thunbergia* climbs by twining

and needs support to climb. Black-eyed Susan vine grows easily from seed and germinates in 14 to 21 days. It sprouts quicker when temperatures are 70° to 75° F. and takes approximately 60 days to bloom. It can be started indoors 4 to 6 weeks before the last expected frost in your area.

Trachelospermum (trak-ee-lo-SPERM-um) *Trachelospermum jasminoides,* star jasmine, Confederate star jasmine; *Trachelospermum asiaticum,* yellow star jasmine; TP, F, E, ◐ ● ○

Zones: T. asiaticum, 8 to 10; *T. jasminoides,* 9 to 10
Height: 15 feet or more
Colors: White, yellow
Characteristics: Although *Trachelospermum* are not true jasmine (see *Jasminum,* page 57), their wonderful scent accounts for their common name of jasmine. Star jasmine weaves a tight, dense mat as it climbs. I have seen it clothe the trunks of

large trees in the South with its 3-inch-long, dark leaves, blooming in shade and completely hiding the tree's bark. The small, pinwheel-shaped blossoms are sweetly fragrant, scenting the air around them. The flowers quickly wither on the vine rather than falling to the ground, but are not unsightly for long as they disappear. 'Madison' is a selection that is hardy to Zone 7.

Trachelospermum asiaticum, a light yellow, won't grow as tall as star jasmine, but it has a cinnamon fragrance that gains in intensity as evening approaches. The oval leaves are pointed, leathery and glossy, providing the perfect backdrop for the flowers. Yellow star jasmine can be grown outdoors as a groundcover, up trellises, around trees, on fences or walls—anywhere the fragrance will be enjoyed or where outdoor lights reflect the pale flowers at night. In hanging baskets yellow star jasmine trails prettily over the edges. In large pots backed by a trellis, it will climb.

Cultural Information: Although both *Trachelosperm* vines need some sun, indoors they tolerate a minimum of 4 hours of direct sun in winter. Planted outdoors they prefer moist, but well-drained, compost-rich soil. When planting, tie the stems to a heavy support to get them started. They will then take off and climb in their own disorderly and compact way up the support. Try growing *Trachelospermum* as a groundcover; just trim the upward-pointing stems. These vines are easy to propagate from stem cuttings.

Trachelospermum jasminoides is shown here growing along wires and pruned into diamond shapes.

They grow slowly at first, faster once their roots are established. If you grow them in pots, you may use any packaged potting soil. Let the plants dry to the touch between waterings. Fertilize every few months. If the leaves begin to yellow, this signals a need for fertilizer.

Tropaeolum (tro-pe-O-lum) *Tropaeolum majus*, nasturtium; *Tropaeolum peregrinum*, canary-bird flower, canary nasturtium; A, F, ○ ◑

Height: T. majus, 6 to 10 feet; T. peregrinum, 10 to 15 feet
Colors: Yellow, orange, red, copper, salmon, pink, scarlet
Characteristics: Brightly colored and tartly fragrant, single or double nasturtium flowers bloom profusely all summer on a plant that almost thrives on neglect. The round, brightly colored flowers have long spurs. Too-rich soil discourages blooming. Both the leaves and flowers are edible and are often used in salads to add their peppery flavor. The round leaves are 1½ to 2½ inches across, like miniature lily pads, and are nice as a garnish for cheese platters.

Tropaeolum majus 'Fordhook Favorite' (named after the Burpee family home) is a vigorous climber with single flowers. All nasturtiums grow quickly and can even be grown indoors as houseplants to bloom throughout the winter in hanging baskets, as long as they have at least 4 hours of sunlight a day. Like birds on the wing, the frilled and fringed, yellow, 1-inch-long flowers with green curved spurs of canary creeper sit along the vine. This is an odd, but pretty, flower. The leaves are gray-green, lobed and shaped like an open palm. They too are edible, with a peppery flavor like that of their cousins, the nasturtiums.
Cultural Information: Tropaeolum grow naturally from Mexico to Peru. Though they tolerate dry soil for a short time, they require thorough watering during prolonged hot, dry periods. They will grow in most well-drained soils, but prefer it on the sandy side. Do not fertilize as it encourages lush, green foliage but few flowers. The seeds are large and easy to plant, quick to germinate and therefore a good choice for a child's garden. Seeds are best sown where they are to grow, as nasturtiums don't transplant well. Cover the seeds completely, as they like darkness to germinate. For climbing rather than sprawling plants, it is necessary to tie the vines to their supports. If you're starting them indoors, plant them in peat pots so you won't disturb the roots when you plant them outdoors. Set them in a warm place (65° to 70° F.); they will germinate in approximately 7 to 12 days, and bloom in about 50 days. Start them indoors 4 to 6 weeks before the last expected frost. The plants can be planted outdoors after all danger of frost. They will often reseed themselves, and have naturalized in southern California.

Trumpet creeper; see *Campsis*

The flowers of the annual vine Tropaeolum peregrinum, *commonly called canary-bird flower, do look as though they could fly.*

Tropaeolum majus *'Fordhook's Finest' is a nasturtium that can climb to 10 feet.*

Vinca major *is a tender-leaved vine often used as a trailing plant for containers.*

Wisteria floribunda alba *(pictured on the right) has white 12-inch clusters of flowers. W. f. 'Rosea' (on the left) has pink clusters 18 inches long.*

Trumpet vines; see *Campsis*

Vinca (VIN-ka) *Vinca major*, vinca, P, E, ● ◗ ○

Zones: 8 to 10, 7 with winter protection
Height: To 5 feet
Color: Lavender-blue
Characteristics: Vinca major 'Variegata' looks a little like ivy, and it is most often grown as a trailing plant for window boxes, hanging baskets and outdoor tubs in areas where frost is a possibility. It is a tender-leaved vine that will be killed by freezing temperatures, although it has lived for many years in an exposed spot in my Zone 7 garden. It easily adapts to being grown indoors as a houseplant over the winter. Each of the individual leaves is edged with a whitish-yellow rim that sparkles in the sunlight. Vinca grows considerably faster than ivy. By summer's end, if conditions are favorable, vines in second-storey window boxes reach the ground, like Rapunzel letting down her hair. One summer, vinca growing in a second-storey window box hung down over the kitchen door in a curtain of vines. We had to part them to walk in and out. (I was reminded of the Chinese beaded curtains that give privacy to mysterious back rooms.) These die back each winter and have continued to flourish each summer, and I haven't had to replace them.
Cultural Information: Vinca is easy to grow. It tolerates poor soils, but grows best in moist soils enriched with organic matter. Propagate by cuttings any time, or by division in the spring.

Virginia creeper; see *Parthenocissus quinquefolia*

Wintercreeper; see *Euonymus*

Winter jasmine; see *Jasminum*

Wisteria (wis-TEE-ree-a) *Wisteria senensis*, **Chinese wisteria;** *Wisteria floribunda*, **Japanese wisteria;** P, F, D, ○ ◗
Zones: Japanese wisteria, 3 to 10; Chinese wisteria, 4 to 10
Height: 20 feet or more
Color: Various shades of purple, white and pink
Characteristics: Beloved and best known of all vines is wisteria, blooming in spring or early summer. There are two native American species, and another ten Asian species. The most popular varieties are the Japanese and the Chinese. They climb buildings and trees to great heights, developing massive, woody trunks as they go. For this reason they are often trained as standards, shaped like trees. They can also be pruned into bushy shrubs. These vines are members of the pea family, and the resemblance can be seen in the sweet pea–shaped flowers hanging in pendulous clusters, or racemes. They produce long flattened pods and are deciduous in the winter.

The Japanese wisteria (*Wisteria floribunda*) is a favorite, with violet flowers borne in racemes 1 to 1½ feet long that bloom in sequence from top to bottom, all the while emitting a sweet fragrance. The velvety green seed pods are from 2 to 6 inches long. A white variety, *W. f. alba*, with 12-inch clusters of flowers, is also available. Another variety, *W. f. macrobotrys*, blooms with reddish-violet racemes 2 to 3 feet long, or longer. 'Rosea's pink clusters are 18 inches long, and 'Issai' has deep blue, 12-inch clusters.

The Chinese wisteria (*Wisteria senensis*) differs from the Japanese wisteria in that it has larger leaves, and only faintly fragrant flowers in racemes generally shorter than a foot in length. There is a white variety, and an especially fragrant variety named *W. s. 'Jako'*. One of the unexplainable quirks of nature is that Chinese wisteria winds left to right, while the Japanese variety twines right to left.

New plants take years to bloom when grown from cuttings, grafting or layering. Seven years is not unusual. If grown from seed, the delay can be even longer. If your wisteria has been grafted, prune off any shoots growing from below the graft. They are of a different, and usually inferior, variety. Plant wisteria only near strong structures or large trees. It hugs like a boa constrictor, and could easily strangle a small tree. A wisteria needs large supports. We attached a wooden beam to the outside of our house, below the second-storey windows, to hold it. One warm winter day, after the vine had grown for a few years, we detached the long, 12-foot stems from the side of the house and removed the weak, thin stems, leaving three main stems. We pruned away all the lower branches and leaves, in order to train the vine to branch at the second storey. Then we braided the main stems, just as I braid my daughter's hair. It took two of us to braid them, a May dance of sorts, as we climbed up and over one stem while holding another. When we finished, the braided stems were retied to the beam. As the years have passed, the stems have grown together, but the braided design remains.

Cultural Information: Wisteria prefer a garden soil rich in compost or organic matter. It likes to be sheltered from strong winds. Plant the pot-grown varieties a foot from their supports, and tie them there to encourage them in the direction they are to grow. It helps to mulch the vine until it gets established, to keep it from drying out. Mature vines can be encouraged to bloom more profusely by pinching back side shoots. Prune after flowering in

Wisteria can be trained to grow as a shrub, or as a small tree, as shown here in the Brooklyn Botanic Garden's rock garden.

early summer and again in winter, to keep the vine in shape and encourage more flowers. If an older vine doesn't bloom, withhold fertilizer; too much nitrogen can cause the growth of leaves at the expense of flowers. By root pruning or hacking off a large root or two, an older vine that has stopped blooming can sometimes be coerced into blooming again.

Woodbine; see *Parthenocissus quinquefolia*

Woody nightshade; see *Solanum*

Yellow star jasmine; see *Trachelospermum*

PESTS AND DISEASES

Vines have adapted to living in over-crowded conditions by reaching for the sky. Made of sturdy stuff, they are easy to grow and usually are not bothered by many pests or diseases. Understanding a vine's needs often prevents problems before they start. Whether your plant has a virtually unquenchable thirst or prefers to let the soil dry out completely between waterings is important to know for the health of your plant. Perhaps it needs protection from wind, more sun or a little shade. In any case, you should make it your business to find out.

Remove any dead branches when you first notice them. This is where disease can easily start, and if you don't check closely, the disease may be rampant before you notice it on other branches. Check for any signs of furry mealy bugs, crawling aphids and jumping whiteflies on new vines before planting them in the garden or taking them into the house. Be sure to inspect regularly between the branches of vines with dense growth. It is easier to control pests or disease when you catch them early. While these are general guidelines for caring for all vines, there are some exceptions. Treat each vine as the individual it is. The particular needs of vines are discussed in the cultural information sections at the end of each plant portrait.

Warfare: Chemical or Natural?

Our preference at Burpee has always been for the natural controls. We have watched chemicals arrive on the market, touted as miracle controls for this pest or that disease, only later to learn the chemicals were endangering our environment. After many years, we noted the appearance of stronger bugs that were resistant to the "miracle control" chemicals. Chemicals do kill pests for a time, but they also hurt the beneficial insects that nature has provided for a balanced environment. So, at Burpee we work with nature first.

Biodegradable products made by Safer, Inc., and Ringers were developed to replace petrochemical-based insecticides, fungicides and miticides. Try these first. Some old-fashioned remedies also work well. Use a spray of 1 tablespoon vinegar to ½ gallon of water, or 1 tablespoon baking soda to 1 gallon of water, for treating mold and powdery mildew. If you need more help or have a severe problem, consult your county extension service for the latest, most up-to-date information on controls for your area.

The entrance to an orchard is covered with 'Scarlett O'Hara' morning glories.

DISEASES

Botrytis: Another name for botrytis is "gray mold blight," a pretty good description of what to look for. Caused by humid conditions, it can be controlled by good air circulation, good sanitation and prompt removal of any vine's diseased parts, to avoid spreading. Safer's Garden Fungicide can be used as a preventative.

Leaf Spot: This occurs most often in humid or wet weather. Spots of various colors (red, brown, yellow) appear. Sometimes, the spots drop out as they dry, leaving holes in the foliage. Remove the infected foliage and put it in the trash, to avoid spreading the disease, which is transmitted by rain, dew, soil, seeds and gardeners. Keep soil around the affected vine moist, but not wet, and avoid overhead watering if leaf spot has been a problem. Don't work in a wet garden, especially with diseased plants; this is when the disease is most likely to be spread.

Powdery Mildew: When powdery mildew is present, the plants look as though they are covered with a dirty, white dust. Not only is it unattractive, but it causes leaves to curl and dry out, and buds to die before blooming. By giving vines good air circulation, watering only in the morning, directly on the soil without wetting the plant foliage, problems can be kept to a minimum. However, some plants such as garden phlox are extremely susceptible. Safer's Garden Fungicide is a good preventative that doesn't leave a noticeable residue.

Rust: Cool, damp nights and humid days encourage rust. Rust is visible in raised and discolored (yellow, reddish or orange) spots that appear on the underside of leaves, causing them to wither. To avoid or discourage rust, do not overwater, avoid overhead watering and remove infected leaves.

Wilt: The cause of wilt may be one of two factors. It may be a physiological problem, where vines wilt from lack of water in the soil, or it may be a pathological problem, caused by fungi plugging the water-conducting tissue in the roots and stems of the vine. The symptoms are the same: a droopy plant with downward-curling leaves. If it is a physiological problem, the water channels in the leaves and stem quit working and go limp. The vine can be expected to recover and regain its stiffness when watered, unless it has been dry for too long, in which case it will die. To avoid this, water regularly and deeply, and fertilize to promote vigorous growth.

When the problem is pathological, caused by fungal wilt, the vine can't recover, even when watered, because the water-conducting tubes are blocked. Clematis wilt is similar to other wilts in effect. It is a common problem that will probably affect your clematis if you plant a number of them. However, it need not kill the clematis, and usually it affects only young vines. There is no way to stop it once it starts, but if a clematis' stem is planted 2 to 3 inches deeper in the ground than it was in the pot it was purchased in, the vine will have the ability to send up new shoots from the underground stem.

INSECTS

Spider Mite

Spider Mites: If you discover tiny red spots on the underside of your vine's leaves, you might think your plant has the measles. It is almost certainly an attack of spider mites. They pierce the leaves and suck out the plant's juices, causing the leaves to yellow, wither and fall off. Wash affected plants with a strong spray of cold water, or spray with an organic insecticide to help control them. Ladybugs are spider mites' natural enemy, and can be purchased from the Burpee catalogue and shipped to you so you can release them onto your plants.

Aphids: Their method of damaging plants is similar to that of spider mites but, in addition, when they suck out the plant's juices, they can introduce infection and spread disease from one plant to another. Aphids are soft-bodied, pear-shaped multicolored insects. Although they are quite small, they're usually not difficult to see because they arrive in mobs. A strong spray of water or an organic insecticide will help to dispel and destroy them.

Beetles: There are many different kinds of beetles (Mexican bean beetles, Japanese beetles, flea beetles, Colorado

Japanese beetle

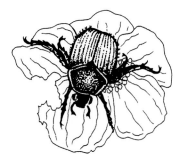

Beetle

potato beetles, cucumber beetles) that, depending on what part of the country you live in and what vegetables and flowers you grow, might appear to plague your vines. The Japanese beetle is the greatest terror, because it eats almost anything: leaves, flowers, grass and fruit. Japanese beetles snuck ashore in 1916, hidden in the soil of nursery stock arriving from the Orient. Presently they live east of the Mississippi, but they continue to move westward. They live for 30 to 40 days, laying their eggs to hatch in the soil, where the larvae proceed to eat the roots of grass for about 4 months. The larvae hibernate over winter and emerge as adult beetles in the summer, to continue the cycle.

Prevention: Beetles are, for the most part, slow moving, and they can easily be flicked off leaves into a jar half-filled with water, where they will drown. There are also natural insecticides available that can be sprayed on affected plants. Beetles can and should be treated while in their grub stage, living in the soil and feeding on the roots of grass. Ringer's grub attack kills by infecting grubs with milky spore disease, caused by *bacillus popilliae*, the naturally occurring active ingredient. Grubs stop feeding and die, releasing billions of new spores to kill other grubs. A single application continues to work for 10 or more years.

Leafhoppers: Wedge-shaped small and green, gray or yellow in color, leafhoppers suck juices from the vine and leave

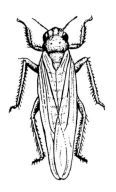

Leafhopper

it with discolored yellow leaves, stunted growth, and buds that do not blossom. They are also carriers of plant diseases, particularly yellows. Fortunately, ladybugs, green lacewings and praying mantises love leafhoppers for dinner. All these insects can be purchased through the mail from Burpee and released at the base of your plants. An insecticidal soap used early in the day when the insects are less active will rid the plant of leafhoppers. It is best to use the soap every few days until you're sure the pests are gone.

Whitefly: Whiteflies grow to 1/16 of an inch, and they have very large white wings for their size. They suck leaves, which

Whiteflies

turn yellow and eventually fall off. This is a common problem on vines grown indoors or wintered over in the house. Safer's insecticidal soap will help. As a prevention, yellow pest strips coated with oil attract whitefly; the whiteflies stick to them and can't move. This is a fairly effective and pleasant way to control numbers of whitefly if you manage to hang the strips discreetly out of sight. A good breeze will blow the pests away.

Mites: Eight-legged and borderline-microscopic, mites are easily located by their webs on the underside of leaves. Mites suck moisture and chlorophyll from the leaves, leaving them yellow and wrinkled. Spray or rub with a soapy solution. Safer's insecticidal soap is best, but 2 tablespoons of dishwashing liquid can be mixed with a gallon of water and used carefully; it must be washed away completely after treatment, to avoid damaging the leaves. Repeat every few days until the mites are gone. A forceful spray of water directed at the underside of leaves weekly will control mites.

Mealy Bugs: Mealy bugs look like furry dots of white cotton balls, ⅛ to ¼ inch across. They are found in all parts of the United States. In California alone there are 193 different known species. They are serious pests outdoors in warm climates and persist as a problem wherever vines are grown indoors. They infest all parts of the vine, above and below ground, and usually cluster around hard-to-reach spots. Nodes, under buds and on the underside of leaves seem to be their favorite sites. They suck out the plant juices, causing wilted leaves, bud drop and loss of fruit. They reproduce monthly and can be persistent pests. Ants are attracted to the sweet, sticky honeydew mealybugs excrete and will carry them to new plants.

Indoors it may be practical to wipe mealy bugs off the plant using a cotton swab dipped in rubbing alcohol, but outdoors that may be too big a job. Chemical insecticide use has left us with mealy bugs that are insecticide-resistant. Insecticidal soaps and oil sprays will reduce their populations. Use green lacewings to control mealybugs, too. They can be ordered through the mail, and are available through the Burpee catalog. If a plant is severely infected, however, it must be disposed of. To avoid mealy bugs, inspect all new plants carefully before you add them to your garden or indoor collections. Once you detect a problem, quarantine any infected plants, to prevent them from infecting other plants, until the mealy bugs are no longer present. Control the ants that spread the mealybugs.

Leaves damaged by the following pests: beetles, flea beetles, caterpillars, aphids and leafhoppers (left to right).

SLUGS AND SNAILS

If they were entered side by side in a beauty contest, the snails would win because their ugly, slimy, wormlike bodies are hidden by shells. Snails and slugs both emerge at night or after a rain to devour foliage. They live in mulch and garden waste, and have no trouble climbing the sides of planters to reach the plants. The brave can pick them off and squash or step on them. The rest of us simply need to spread diatomaceous earth (ground, fossilized aquatic plants, available commercially in bags) around the base of plants. Slugs and snails hate crawling through rough soil, which scratches their smooth skin, and diatomaceous earth is extremely uncomfortable for them. It must be reapplied after rainfall.

Snail

Slug

GARDENERS' MOST-ASKED QUESTIONS

The first Burpee catalogue was mailed in 1876, and the catalogues have been coming ever since, offering gardeners a wealth of seeds, plants, fruits, shrubs and trees, as well as hints and advice for better gardening. From the early years to today, Burpee has received many letters from customers describing their gardens or asking questions about how better to grow their plants. We have selected the most frequently asked questions about vines, and answer them in this book.

Question: *What vines grow in the shade?*

Answer: Many vines, flowering and fruiting, grow in partial shade; there are fewer for dense shade. Gauge the amount of shade in the area where you want to plant first. If the area receives approximately 4 hours of direct sun, it is in partial shade. Dense shade means some dappled sun but fewer hours of direct sun. This does make a difference. Many of the vines listed for sun will tolerate a half day or 6 hours of sun. The denser the shade, the fewer the vines that will grow well under those conditions. In the Plant Portraits, you will find vines are noted for shade and part shade. Clematis likes part shade, and English ivy, climbing hydrangea, Boston ivy, Virginia creeper, vinca and *Euonomus* all thrive in part shade or dense shade.

PLANNING

Question: *Which are the best evergreen vines to grow?*

Answer: It depends on the area of the country you live in. English ivy, akebia, winter creeper and vinca will grow in most parts of the country. For frost-free areas there is a large selection. Check the USDA plant hardiness map (pages 90–91) to see which zone you live in, then look in the plant portrait chapter for vines appropriate for your area.

Question: *Are there any vines with edible fruit that are attractive enough for me to include in my flower garden?*

Answer: Try hardy kiwi and grapes. Scarlet runner beans and hyacinth beans are edible and may be included in a vegetable or flower garden. I also like Jack-Be-Little pumpkins, which grow on short vines. Refer to the *Burpee American Gardening Series: Vegetables* for cultural information and varieties.

Question: *Which vines will cover an ugly landscape feature or quickly screen an area?*

Answer: For a quick-covering perennial vine, try English ivy, porcelain berry, honeysuckle or silver lace vine. For a temporary fix, use an annual vine such as morning glory, moonflower, scarlet runner bean or hyacinth bean.

On the author's back arbor, three climbing roses twine together: pink 'Aloha', yellow 'Golden Showers', and orange and yellow 'Joseph's Coat'. 'Simplicity', a shrub rose, is in the foreground.

POPULAR CLIMBERS AND THEIR HEIGHTS

Height	Rose Type
Climbers reaching 5 to 10 feet	'Aloha'
	'America'
	'Don Juan'
	'Eden Climber'
	'Golden Showers'
	'Joseph's Coat'
	'Margo Koster'
	'Rhonda'
Climbers and Ramblers reaching 10 to 20 feet	'Blaze Improved'
	'Climbing Étoile de Hollande'
	'Climbing Peace'
	'Constance Spry'
	'Dortmund'
	'Gloire de Dijon'
	'New Dawn'
	'Zéphirine Drouhin'
Climbers and Ramblers reaching 20 feet and above	'Bobbie James'
	'Belvedere'
	'Excelsa'
	'Kiftsgate'
	'Lawrence Johnston'
	'Leontine Gervais'
	'Paul's Himalayan Musk Rambler'

Question: *Which vines flower for the longest period of time?*

Answer: Annual vines usually take several months before they start to flower. When they bloom they continue to produce flowers for many months, until they are hit by hard frost in northern climates. Some annuals such as morning glory bloom year 'round in the tropics. A number of tropical vines, among them plumbago, allamanda and mandevilla, also bloom year 'round when planted outdoors, taking a short rest when grown indoors in greenhouses. Other perennial vines for northern climates with summerlong bloom are honeysuckles, some climbing roses and many clematis.

Question: *I would like to plant a climbing rose against the house. How high should the trellis be?*

Answer: Climbing roses, available in various colors and "shapes," will reach different heights. Some of the most popular climbers and their heights are shown in the box on the left.

Question: *What is the difference between a vine and a groundcover?*

Answer: In many cases it is only the way in which the plant is grown. Without a structure to climb, a number of vines grow prostrate and make excellent groundcovers. Many vines have naturalized along roadsides and hold banks as groundcovers. Some, such as five-leaf akebia, porcelain vine, bittersweet and *Lonicera japonica halliana*, I wouldn't recommend as a groundcover in the home garden—unless there is room to spare—because they become invasive. Vines recommended for use as groundcovers include *Clematis maximowicziana, Clematis montana, Clematis virginiana, Euonymus radicans, Hedera helix, Lathyrus latifolius, Parthenocissus quinquefolia, Parthenocissus tricuspidata, Plumbago capensis, Tropaeolum majus,* and *Vinca major.*

GROWING

Question: *I'm a beginning gardener and would like to grow the easiest flowering vines. Are there many?*

Answer: Most of the vines included in this book are easy to grow. Any of the quick-growing annuals such as morning glory, balloon vine and nasturtium would be a good place to start. Perennial favorites such as honeysuckle, fleece vine and trumpet vine are also easygoing.

Question: *Which clematis are the easiest to grow?*

Answer: The sweet-smelling species, or small-flowered, clematis are easier to grow than the large-flowered clematis. For spring bloom grow *Clematis montana,* and for fall bloom, *Clematis maximowicziana,* the sweet autumn clematis.

PROBLEMS

Question: *My* Actinidia kolomikta *'Arctic Beauty' vine's leaves are green with no variegation at all. What's wrong?*
Answer: The variegation of kolomikta vine improves with age and exposure to sunlight. Give it time and a sunny location, and it should provide you with 4 to 8 weeks of green foliage splashed with white and pink from spring to early summer.

Question: *My trumpet vine has never bloomed, what's wrong?*
Answer: Trumpet vines can take 5 years before they are established enough to bloom. They should bloom reliably once they are established in a sunny location with reasonably fertile soil. If there is too much shade on them, they might wait until their tops are in the sun before blooming.

Question: *An old wisteria vine growing on the side of our house has beautiful foliage but hasn't bloomed for several years. Is there anything I can do?*
Answer: Don't fertilize the vine. Too much nitrogen can accelerate growth of the leaves at the expense of flowers. Root pruning, hacking off a large root or two on an older vine, can sometimes shock the plant into blooming again.

Question: *I planted a climbing hydrangea 2 years ago and it hasn't grown, nor has it flowered. Does it need fertilizer?*
Answer: It takes about 3 years for climbing hydrangea to establish a vigorous root system. Even though it looks as though the vine hasn't grown, it has been growing underground. Once the roots are established the vine will grow quickly. Don't use a high-nitrogen fertilizer; instead, bone meal will help root growth.

Question: *My American bittersweet has never produced berries. What is wrong with it?*
Answer: Female plants produce berries, so a male plant must be present for pollination. You probably have all-female or all-male plants.

PRUNING

Question: *How should I prune a clematis?*
Answer: Not all clematis are pruned the same way. Pruning depends on when the clematis blooms and whether it blooms on old wood or new wood. See page 47 for information on the three categories of clematis and how to prune them.

Please also write or call for a free Burpee catalog:

W. Atlee Burpee & Company
300 Park Avenue
Warminster, PA 18974
215-674-9612

THE USDA PLANT HARDINESS MAP OF NORTH AMERICA

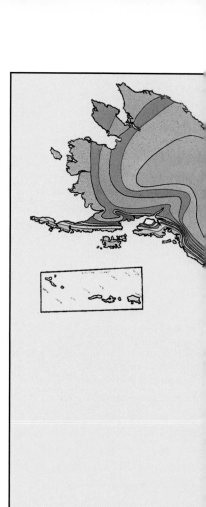

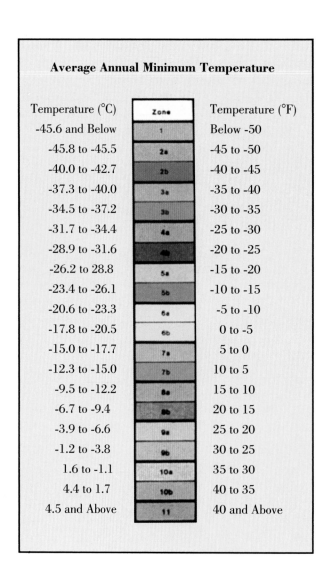

Average Annual Minimum Temperature

Temperature (°C)	Zone	Temperature (°F)
-45.6 and Below	1	Below -50
-45.8 to -45.5	2a	-45 to -50
-40.0 to -42.7	2b	-40 to -45
-37.3 to -40.0	3a	-35 to -40
-34.5 to -37.2	3b	-30 to -35
-31.7 to -34.4	4a	-25 to -30
-28.9 to -31.6	4b	-20 to -25
-26.2 to 28.8	5a	-15 to -20
-23.4 to -26.1	5b	-10 to -15
-20.6 to -23.3	6a	-5 to -10
-17.8 to -20.5	6b	0 to -5
-15.0 to -17.7	7a	5 to 0
-12.3 to -15.0	7b	10 to 5
-9.5 to -12.2	8a	15 to 10
-6.7 to -9.4	8b	20 to 15
-3.9 to -6.6	9a	25 to 20
-1.2 to -3.8	9b	30 to 25
1.6 to -1.1	10a	35 to 30
4.4 to 1.7	10b	40 to 35
4.5 and Above	11	40 and Above

This zone map provides a broad outline of various temperature zones in North America. However, every garden has its own microclimate.

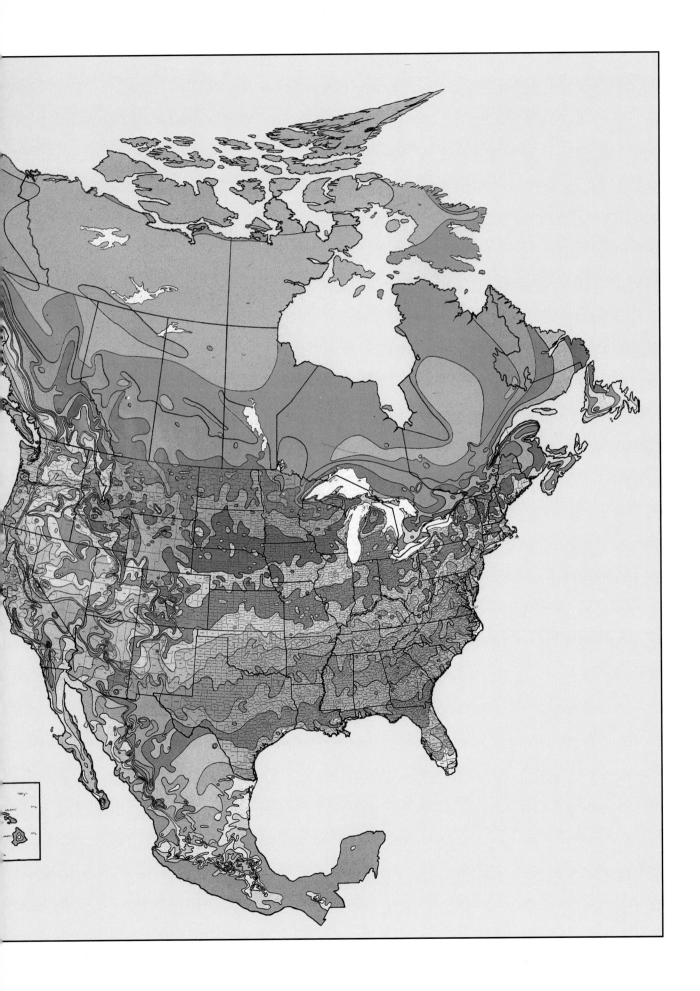

Index

Macmillan Gardening and the W. Atlee Burpee Company
are pleased to extend to readers of the
Burpee American Gardening Series these special offers:

Cut along dotted line.

Burpee American Gardening Series Readers:
Save $3.00
with This Exclusive Offer!

There are lots of good reasons why thousands of gardeners order their seeds, bulbs, plants and other gardening supplies from the Burpee Gardens Catalogue: highest quality products, informed and courteous service, and a guarantee on which you can depend.

Now there's another good reason: you can save $3.00 on an order of $10.00 or more from the Burpee Gardens Catalogue. This is an exclusive offer available only to readers of the Burpee American Gardening Series. Just enclose this coupon with your order and deduct $3.00 from the total where indicated on the order form from your catalogue.

If you need a Catalogue just send in the coupon below.

Your signature _____

This discount coupon must accompany your order.

This offer is not transferable. No photocopies or facsimiles of the coupon will be accepted. Coupon has no cash value and may not be redeemed for cash or exchanged for products at retail stores. Offer void where prohibited, taxed or otherwise restricted.

FREE!
Gardening's Most Wanted Catalogue!

Start your garden or expand it with high quality products from Burpee. The Burpee Gardens Catalogue features seeds, bulbs and plants for new varieties of flowers and vegetables as well as hundreds of old favorites and a broad range of garden supplies. Send in this coupon today to:

W. Atlee Burpee & Company
300 Park Avenue
Warminster, PA 18974

Please send me a free Burpee Gardens Catalogue.

Name _____

Street _____

City _____ State _____ Zip _____

Cut along dotted line.